YUTOPIAN

In situ anthropomorphic Candelaria sherd from Estructura Uno, eager to tell its story.

THE WILLIAM & BETTYE NOWLIN SERIES
in Art, History, and Culture of the Western Hemisphere

YUTOPIAN

Archaeology, Ambiguity and the Production of Knowledge in Northwest Argentina

JOAN M. GERO

University of Texas Press Austin

Requests for permission to reproduce material from this work should be sent to:
    Permissions
    University of Texas Press
    P.O. Box 7819
    Austin, TX 78713-7819
    http://utpress.utexas.edu/index.php/rp-form

♾ The paper used in this book meets the minimum requirements of ANSI/NISO Z39.48-1992
(R1997) (Permanence of Paper).

Library of Congress Cataloging-in-Publication Data

Gero, Joan M., author.
    Yutopian : archaeology, ambiguity, and the production of knowledge in Northwest Argentina
/ Joan M. Gero. — First edition.
    pages   cm — (The William and Bettye Nowlin series in art, history, and culture of the
Western Hemisphere)
    Includes bibliographical references.
    ISBN 978-0-292-77201-4 (cloth : alk. paper) — ISBN 978-0-292-77202-1 (pbk. : alk. paper) —
ISBN 978-1-4773-0394-8 (library e-book) — ISBN 978-1-4773-0395-5 (non-library e-book)
    1. Catamarca (Argentina : Province)—Antiquities. 2. Argentina, Northwest—Antiquities.
3. Excavations (Archaeology)—Argentina. 4. Indians of South America—Argentina—Catamarca (Province)—Antiquities. 5. Community archaeology—Argentina. 6. Archaeology—
Fieldwork. I. Title. II. Series: William & Bettye Nowlin series in art, history, and culture of
the Western Hemisphere.
    F2821.1.C3G47 2015
    982'.45—dc23   2014047158
    doi:10.7560/772014

Facts

"Zurich is in the Alps" I learned
  that, and had a fact. But I thought the Alps
  were in South America. Then I learned
  that's the Andes — the Alps were somewhere
  else. And Zurich is famous, for something.

So I gave up fact and went to myth:
Zurich is the name of a tropical bird that
whets its bill on the ironwood tree in South America
singing about life and how good facts are.
The Alps are a people who raise reindeer, somewhere else.

Then it became important that the moon be
a close friend. I wanted the wind
always to make that same sound, sustaining
us through all the seasons, and always
around us — the night, and then the world.

Moons have changed many times by now,
and the wind has a voice more peremptory. Clear
nights have deepened all the way to the stars.
Zurich is famous and far from here,
And there isn't enough room for all the facts —
In this world.

WILLIAM STAFFORD

Contents

Contents

Contents

Contents

Figures

STARTING TO DIG

ESTRUCTURA DOS

ESTRUCTURA UNO

ESTRUCTURA TRES

INTERPRETING NÚCLEO UNO

ESTRUCTURA ONCE AND THE ISSUE OF REMODELING HOUSES

ESTRUCTURA CUATRO

UNDERSTANDING YUTOPIAN AS AN EARLY FORMATIVE SETTLEMENT

DATA FROM THE EXPERTS

CARDONAL BY COMPARISON

WRAP-UPS AND POSTSCRIPTS

Tables

Acknowledgments

At the heart of this book stand Jorge Chaile and his family who own Yutopian and who housed us and cared for us for many years; their innumerable generosities and kindnesses, diligent work and insightful understanding of archaeology and archaeologists have made this study possible. I thank them humbly and gratefully and daily. Most sincere gratitude also goes to Álvaro and Federico Chaile for their fine contributions to the project and beyond. It has been a great pleasure not only to participate in the intimacies of the tiny community of Yutopian but also to share experiences with many people of the larger Valle del Cajón, and I hope my appreciation and fondness have made themselves clear for the Aroaz family in Lagunita, Ramona Chaile and her children in San José, the Pachaos in Ovejería, Marcos Chayle and Julia Vargas de Chayle in La Quebrada, and so many other *lugareños* who taught and gave us so much. In Santa María, we are so lucky and appreciative of friends like Noemi Rodriguez and Mario Caserez; we still mourn Mario's premature death.

The work at Yutopian and Cardonal was conducted under the auspices—and with the kind assistance—of officials in Santa María, especially Rubén Quiroga, Director of the Museo Provincial Arqueológico "Eric Boman." At the provincial level we recognize the help of the Catamarca Dirección General de Antropología, especially Carlos Nazar. The municipalities of San José and Santa María generously provided transport into the field, and the town of Santa María allowed us to use their camping facilities as our laboratory; they have also stored our artifacts. South Carolina Electric and Gas generously provided the solar panels to Yutopian. Sincere thanks to Dr. Terence D'Altroy for the generous loan, in 1996, of his state-of-the-art total station mapping equipment, along with his field crew trained to use it. Cristina Scattolin's superb skills in mapping and identifying ceramics were critical to the success of the project.

Patricia Escolar provided invaluable assistance with the visual identification of obsidians from different quarry sites and generously consulted with the project about Formative lithics on several occasions; Marisa Lazzari analyzed Yutopian's obsidian samples. Guillermo Mengoni kindly loaned his expertise to evaluating Yutopian's faunal samples before Andrés Izeta joined in the project. Pamela Vandiver of the Smithsonian Conservation Analytical Laboratory analyzed the scoria from Yutopian, and Ron Hatfield at Beta Analytic recalibrated the C14 dates, many initially run 16 years earlier. Alejandro Haber and his students at the Universidad Nacional de Catamarca Escuela de Arqueología taught me a great deal and helped the project in innumerable ways. It was a privilege to communicate with Mr. Gene Titmus (1936–2010) of Jerome, Idaho, about stone tools from Yutopian, and I am sincerely indebted to him for his insightful experimentation on how side-struck flakes were produced.

Financial support to locate and work at the site of Yutopian was provided by the University of South Carolina Research and Productive Scholarship Program, the Josephine Abney Award for gender research (University of South Carolina), the Wenner-Gren Foundation for Anthropological Research International Collaboration Award and supplementary grant, the Fulbright Commission, the Universidad Nacional de Catamarca Escuela de Arqueología and American University's Faculty Research program. For the work at Cardonal, thanks are due to the Heinz Foundation for Latin American Archaeology. I appreciate the logistical support generously provided by the Smithsonian Institution's ASC Program.

Writing was undertaken with generous support at Clare Hall at Cambridge University, the Dumbarton Oaks PreColumbian Library in Washington, DC, the Bald Mountain Writing Center in Fairlee, Vermont, and at the Chauncey Loomis Center for Interdisciplinary Studies in Stockbridge, Massachusetts. I owe enormous thanks to Joanne Pillsbury, Colin McEwan, Bridget Gazzo, Lynne and Bill Fitzhugh, Claudine Scoville and Craig Loomis for enabling and enriching these intellectually stimulating opportunities in some of the loveliest places I have known.

It has been a special delight to work with students on this project: Dante Coronel (1992); Juan Leoni (now Dr.), Laura Pérez-Jimeno, Hugo Puentes, Catherine Heyne, Liliana Arenas (1994); Rachel Campo, Josh Fletcher, Cecilia Fraga, Paul Lewis, Leticia Martinez (now Dra.), Ramón Quinteros (1996); Michael Clem, Lauren Ebin, Rosemary Lyon, Dolores Tobias (1998); Fabiana Bugliani (now Dra.), Ilana Hahnel, Andrés Izeta (now Dr.), Elsa Mabel Mamani, Jessica Streibel (1999); and Jodi Barnes (now Dra.), Ali Ghobadi, Jocelyn Knauf (now Dra.), Lisa Munns, Hide Nishizawa (now Dr.) and Jeremy Walter (2004). Robert Thompson collected and analyzed phytoliths, and Jack Rossen served with grace and humor as ethnobotanist for much of the project. Josh Fletcher and Rachel Campo made special contributions drafting maps and excavation profiles at Yutopian, finalized by Houston Ruck and Jesús Quiroz. I am

Acknowledgments

particularly grateful to Fabiana Bugliani, who drew the ceramic profiles and coauthored Bit 83 about the ceramics from Yutopian; to Andrés Izeta, who coauthored Bit 82 on faunal remains; and to Jack Rossen, who coauthored Bits 79 and 80 on plants and diet. Thanks also to Vicky Surles, who finalized the map of Cardonal. And, finally, I was very lucky to get Helen Langa's icons.

A few "bits" included in this book take shape out of my earlier writings. Bit 2 on knowledge production takes off from a chapter I contributed to *Gender and Archaeology,* edited by Rita Wright (University of Pennsylvania Press, 1996). Bit 3 on ambiguity follows the argument I presented in the *Journal of Archaeological Method and Theory,* vol. 14 (2007), edited by Margaret Conkey and Alison Wylie, and Bit 32, "How the Gendered Household Works," follows an argument I presented (with M. C. Scattolin) in a chapter of *In Pursuit of Gender,* edited by Sarah Milledge Nelson and Myriam Rosen-Ayalon (Altamira Press, 2002). I appreciate permission to revisit those arguments here. Bit 22 on excavation forms was first presented in an archaeology colloquium at Cambridge University in 1990, and Bit 36 uses data compiled by me and Anita Cook for an SAA presentation in 2012. William Stafford's poem "Facts" is reprinted with kind permission from *The Way It Is: New and Selected Poems 1998* (copyright 1993 by William Stafford and the Estate of William Stafford; permission granted by The Permissions Company, Inc., on behalf of Graywolf Press, Minneapolis, Minnesota, www.graywolfpress.org).

The challenges of producing this book were eased, enlightened and made more fun with generous help from unexpected places as well as from dear friends: Catherine Allen, Mitch Allen, Linda Brown, Geoff Burkhardt, Anita Cook, MaryJo Figuerero, Alejandro Haber, Regina Harrison, Hedy Kalmar-Rosenthal, Willy Mengoni, Adriana Muñoz, Tim Murtha, Javier Nastri, Axel Nielsen, Dolores Root, Pamela Vandiver, Brett Williams, and my wonderfully professional editor at the University of Texas Press, Theresa May. I am particularly grateful for the generous, thoughtful and thorough "anonymous" reviews from Benjamin Alberti and Axel Nielsen, whose invaluable comments have often been incorporated wholesale into the text; I couldn't have had better critics and I thank them effusively for their help and their suggested readings. Cristina Scattolin's thoughts and practices are deeply interwoven in much that is presented here, but she is not to be faulted for the writing or interpretations offered.

As always my deepest gratitude, respect and love go to Stephen, chief mood elevator, wind spirit restorer, heart back-up. Thank you inexpressibly for making the book happen and keeping post-book dreams alive. You are my sunshine.

YUTOPIAN

Frameworks

1

INTRODUCTION

During field seasons in 1994, 1996, 1998 and 1999 archaeological teams from the United States and Argentina worked at the site of Yutopian, and additionally in the nearby town of Santa María, to recover and analyze cultural material from what proved to be an unusual Formative period site. The area where we worked, the northwest region of Argentina, comprises the southern end of the Andean chain, and within Argentina it is the mountainous part of the country where traditional lifeways and languages, crops and communities are the least directly impacted by Argentina's modern state apparatus. Many of the joys of the project have come from being able to live and work, if only for short stints of time, among agricultural people who recognize North Americans as being as equally remote as Argentineans who come from the faraway capital city of Buenos Aires: we are all strangers made to feel welcome according to our generosity, with expressions of conversation as well as more material formulations.

The site that this book focuses on, Yutopian, was first occupied during what Argentineans call the Early (or Lower) Formative period, 200 BCE to 500 CE,[1] the period when intensive agriculture and sedentary village life were first practiced in this region. By generalized accounts, differentiated camelids (suggesting domestication) appear in the Argentinean highlands by 2000 BCE (Olivera 2001:94), and corn is identified roughly around 100 BCE (Gil et al. 2006:201). Settlements belonging to this period vary according to the region in which they occur but in general—and particularly in Catamarca where we worked—the settlements are homesteads characterized as replicative, dispersed individual or clustered structures, either freestanding or interspersed among walled agricultural fields and animal corrals; few examples of these have been excavated (Berberián 1989; Gero and Scattolin 2002; Núñez Regueiro 1998; Olivera 2001; Scattolin 1990). Nearby, in the Tafí Valley, domestic sites sometimes include standing worked stones called by their excavators *menhires* (Gonzáles and Núñez Regueiro 1960), although these are otherwise absent at Early Formative sites, and in the Alamito region there are well-published examples of what have been described as Early Formative ceremonial sites composed of circles of mounds with a central patio (Tartusi and Núñez Regueiro 1993).

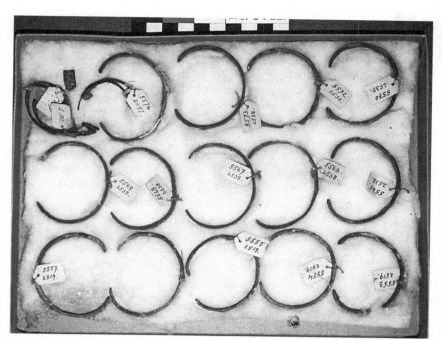

Figure 1. Early Formative bronze bracelets recovered from Laguna Blanca. From the collection of Benjamín Muniz Barreto, Museo de La Plata. Photograph courtesy of Cristina Scattolin.

Throughout the central area of Northwest Argentina, this same period is characterized by the circulation of exotic goods, including complex ceramics such as Condorhuasi polychrome and Candelaria modeled and incised wares, copper and gold ornaments, and bronze bracelets and bells (Fig. 1),[2] although often these elaborated goods lack excavated provenience (Tarragó and Scattolin 1999). It was difficult for us to reconcile the dispersed population settlement pattern and apparent lack of social complexity in the central portion of NOA (Northwest Argentina) with the obvious complexity of circulating manufactured goods that exhibited high investments of productive energy and sometimes rare raw material composition. We defined this apparent paradox as the focus of our research project: identifying sites where some of these goods may have been produced and sites where these elaborated goods were used or consumed, in relation to the supposedly uniform low-density "egalitarian" settlement system. The fact that we ended up working at Yutopian was either the luckiest of coincidences or a wonderful example of finding what you want to find.

Over the years Yutopian proved to be a surprising site for many reasons. Not only was the site unusually well preserved with its living floors apparently abandoned and intact, but it was also a rich source of prehistoric materials, some of which were new to the profession and some of which were newly revealed in Early Formative contexts and arrangements. From such rich data, we can now produce new information about the Early Formative period in Northwest Argentina and the particular site of Yutopian, some of it requiring paradigms to be rewritten and some of it relevant on more local scales: for the first time we can document the presence of established villages in this region during this period; we can describe the organization of Formative production sequences in distinct technological areas; we can show different trans-generational household arrangements as well as the remarkable persistence of agricultural regimes over more than a thousand years. Significantly, we can point to the appearance of new forms of power relations closely intertwined with other social developments and emerging at a time when egalitarian societies are supposed to have predominated.

These archaeological conclusions are among the results reached after we had spent three field seasons at Yutopian, one additional season conducting analysis in Santa María, and a field season at the site of Cardonal. But not surprisingly, as we were working toward new archaeological understandings, we were also learning about how to do archaeology most effectively in this region. For instance, we came to know how our flotation systems needed to be modified by water availability, how to recognize and treat rodent burrows, how the daily morning frosts in July and August changed our field schedule. We also came to know what risks were entailed in our long- and short-term storage arrangements, whom we should employ on the project to accomplish our goals and keep peace in the community, what local materials could be pressed into service when "northern" products or procedures proved inadequate, how the Argentinean permitting system restricted and opened researchers' access to project areas, how to answer questions about why North Americans come to excavate in Argentina.

As we acquired knowledge about doing archaeology at Yutopian, we also became familiar with Andean lifeways more generally; we learned which work tasks are gendered and which are not, what people mean by particular local phrases or gestures, what subjects or actions are never discussed/undertaken by local people, how seasonal schedules of subsistence and ritual obligations are observed, where community leadership lies and how it is defined, how meals are organized, what foods are portable, how settlements and population movement have changed over time, where given resources are gathered and what they were used for, and much more.

Finally, we constantly learned about ourselves as we worked at Yutopian: about how consistent we were able to be in our decisions, whether we operated better giving incisive instructions or preferred a consensual style on the project, who was most affected by hunger or fatigue or cold, with whom we worked well, and what we could and could not tolerate: Messiness/fastidiousness? Obsessiveness/relaxed work modes? Working constantly in two languages? In fact, we learned a lot about our individual strengths and weaknesses in the field. All these areas of new learning were absolutely critical—and inevitable—as the project moved forward; they constituted an intertwined and parallel learning trajectory to gaining archaeological knowledge.

For significant reasons that I explain in the next two "frameworks," I have chosen not to erase these histories of our knowledge making at Yutopian and not to shut out the wonderfully unfamiliar context in which we worked. Here the scientific work is not foregrounded at the expense of obliterating its context, but instead the context (regional, historical, political, intellectual, professional) is recognized as modifying the work at every turn. Possibly because I collaborated very closely with Argentinean archaeologists and archaeology students in this project, and because sometimes we didn't take the same approach to our field studies (see Bit 11, "The positionality of practice"), I recognize that the decisions made in conducting field research (or in any scientific undertaking) play a fundamental role in shaping the knowledge produced in that project. That is, a wide range of considerations and alternate choices ultimately contribute to what we recognize as our knowledge outcomes, and it is not irrelevant that this project was undertaken by a joint US/Argentina research team, nor that I had conducted previous research in other parts of the Andes, nor that I identify as a feminist and that my interests include gendered accounts of the past, nor that my Argentinean collaborator had distinct research interests at the time, nor a host of other things that matter to how we did archaeology at Yutopian. Different researchers, a different research context, different concerns would all produce different knowledges, which does not make our outcomes less trustworthy, only more singular.

The book I've written here explores the venerated genre of archaeological writing called "the monograph," wherein a field researcher reports her methodology and findings on a specific, self-contained project. The conventional format for such a work is highly specified: it begins with an introduction to why the research is important and describes the location of the study area with its topographic features and environmental aspects. Then the methodology employed at the site is offered in more-or-less generalized terms, and the results detailed one area at a time, or more commonly by one raw material class after another. A final section called "Conclusions" and/or "Discussion" ends the work.

While this format for reporting archaeological work served the discipline well for many decades (and I still use some of these conventions), its empirical and atheoretical bias has put it out of favor more recently. Moreover, it leaves out much of interest. The people who worked at the site are invisible; the constantly changing emotional landscape that accompanies hard physical labor with unfamiliar peoples in faraway locations is seldom mentioned; the puzzlement and lack of closure about interpretations and the crucial strategic and methodological decisions we must constantly make are almost never brought up. Painfully, the unfamiliar codes of behavior and expectations between visiting archaeologists and host landowners/land workers—which are constantly being negotiated and redefined—are buried deep beneath the surface accounts of what "happened" and what was "found."

There are many reasons for these omissions. Archaeologists carefully circumscribe what they write about, not just merely to observe page limits and produce books of manageable sizes. And it is not only to keep focused on the archaeology that they regularly omit so much of beauty and interest from their accounts. I believe much of the broader visual, cultural, emotional and intellectual context is kept "off site" because the veracity of archaeological accounts depends on it. Indeed, objectivity, the notion that lies at the heart of science itself, requires that all unique, personal experiences be considered largely irrelevant and removed from consideration; to include emotions or cultural practices discounts the veracity of what was "discovered." Needless to say, I don't accept this view.

This book narrates our investigations, describing the *chaîne opératoire* of research practices employed in collecting data and summarizing the results of our archaeological investigations. If it is a "site report," it has been reconfigured by contemporary interests and understandings. Most notably, I highlight the contingent aspects of the knowledge we are building, how our knowledge depends on and takes form around what was previously known/not known, and how the actions and decisions of specific individuals are closely tied to how this specific knowledge was produced, as opposed to other bodies of knowledge that other investigators might have produced. Personalities, time constraints, convictions and uncertainties all play major roles here.

If the content of this "site report" is odd, so too is the manner in which I have organized it. Although the presentation of material more or less follows the chronological order in which we proceeded, I have tried to distinguish separate threads, with each section, or "Bit," designated as belonging to a particular thread. I lay out a basic chronological "Narrative" that explains our work at each stage of the project, but then intersperse the central narrative with "Arguments," my term for the a priori intellectual positions I brought to the project which colored my understandings and my research decisions; "Episodes" (identifying and describing segments of archaeological fieldwork); "Backstories" (offering background information); "Andean Ways" (relating particularly vivid moments or activities at Yutopian, not as ethnographic parallels but rather to stir the imagination about how lives are lived differently, where other peoples' daily routines and foundational assumptions nudge us to think broadly and creatively in reconstructing prehistoric life); and "Socio-politics" (where we are forced to confront the social, moral, economic, and politic realities of both the immediate and the larger worlds in which we practice archaeology).

The partitions I use are often awkward, partially because everything here is, after all, a narrative of one sort or another, and "Narratives" do not always separate cleanly from "Episodes" while "Socio-politics" admittedly underlie many aspects of work, etc. Taxonomies are always messy. Perhaps the most difficult thread to construct has been the interspersed segments called "Data," where I link summaries of what we actually found and what we learned at Yutopian, making it easy for readers to get a no-nonsense picture of the "results" of our excavations and analysis. This has been especially frustrating because "data" are everywhere, clinging to parts of the narratives at every point and intertwining themselves throughout our observations and procedures. I've done what I can, sometimes separating "raw data" (e.g., numbers) from "descriptive data," and sometimes recognizing the "cooking" of data, but I've also been forced to concede that this thread hardly does justice to all that we learned about Early Formative life from Yutopian. Still other insertions into the basic narrative are not threaded but punctuate the text to draw attention to contingencies that impacted the research. In general it can be seen that narrative and contextual bits figure more heavily in the earlier stages of research while research results (data) congregate in the concluding sections.

One further complication: all the work at Yutopian was conducted by me in conjunction with an Argentinean collaborator, M. Cristina Scattolin of CONICET and the Museo Etnográfico "Juan B. Ambrosetti" as well as the Universidad de Buenos Aires. Lic. Scattolin contributed essential and extensive background knowledge about Formative period sites in the region, offered critical information about ceramic forms and designs and phases, brought wonderful well-trained students to the project, introduced sophisticated and productive archaeological techniques into all phases of work at the site, and suggested constructive and innovative ways of thinking about Yutopian. But Scattolin has since distanced herself from my interpretations of the site in several important regards—some of which I will take up specifically—and declined to collaborate in writing this book. Thus although all credit is due to

Cristina Scattolin and her invaluable contributions to the project, I wish to emphasize that the interpretations put forward here are my own and are not to be attributed to her, as is her wish.

Notes

1. Following current usage, dates here are given as BCE (Before the Common Era) and CE (Common Era) rather than the older form of BC and AD dates.

2. Eighty metal bracelets were collected from La Quebrada by Rodolfo Schreiter and sold in 1930 to Erland Nordenskiöld at the Göteborg Museum in Sweden where they were recently analyzed by Stenborg and Muñoz (1999). See also Muñoz and Fasth (2006).

2

FRAMEWORK

Knowledge production at Yutopian

In earlier work (Gero 1993, 1996) I tried to demonstrate how facts are produced in archaeology, as a strategy for feminist archaeologies but also as a program for challenging the unacknowledged agendas of science. My argument was that if we could identify the part that human agency plays in knowledge production, documenting the stream of human and social elements that science often deliberately obscures, we would open up the process of fact production to alternative ways and voices. This strategy is familiar to feminists who have long raised epistemological questions about how the world is known; we have challenged the arrangements and practices that fix "knowledge" as "science" and argued for recognition of the relationship between the exclusion of women from science and the myth of science as rational and transparent. These commitments lead feminists to pose ontological questions about *what we know*, raising crucial questions about who can be a "knower," about the relationships between the community of knowers and the knowledge they cooperatively produce, and about the moralization of objectivity. Feminists speak of problematizing common understandings—using new ideas to make the everyday world strange.

These related strategies and concerns underpinned our work at Yutopian and provide a framework for this account. Most obviously I am eager to show that what we learned at Yutopian was fundamentally linked to *how* we worked—which itself proceeded from, and directly reflected, our intellectual, social and professional worlds. I sketch my approach here.

In traditional site reports, as in most genres of scientific writing, the history of fact production is either erased from its context of production or cleverly inverted and distorted in ways that make it appear automatic, neutral and transparent, suggesting that anyone excavating the same bit of soil matrix would have "found" what we found and would put forward an account similar to this one. Like other scientists, archaeologists write as though objects, facts, sometimes even laws, are givens, and that such facts and laws merely await the timely revelation of their existence by devoted scholars. Since archaeologists "unearth" our data, literally brushing off the dirt that covered them for centuries, we are inclined to think of our facts as being removed from any human agency that was responsible for having produced them. We merely part the darkness that had kept these truths from being known more generally and had kept us in ignorance, and happening to look where we did, shedding new light on our subjects, we then "found" our answers.

In the constructivist view, however, science is not about "discovery" but about making order out of disorder, about finding the right interpretations or arguments to reduce noise in data, about chains of decisions and negotiations that must be made on the basis of previous decisions (Garfinkle 1967). In this way, researchers build an internally consistent argument or framework that is publicly advanced and that "works" in its own terms and with its own instrumentation, but that can operate *only* in this historically fixed logic rather than being descriptive of any disarticulated, external reality. The knowledge we produce arises directly out of—and is profoundly structured by—the everyday features and practices that we build into, and count on as, "doing archaeology": the assumed, mundane, unquestioned procedures and routines in research, the accepted use of specific tools and instruments, and the carefully inculcated technical abilities that we teach and expect of practitioners. Within this system of shared knowledge, each practical learned and natural-seeming activity is "doubly contextual in being both *context-shaped* and *context-renewing*" (Heritage 1987:242), and the "facts" emerging from such a context (such as at Yutopian) are thoroughly situated within its rules and organization.

But the science (or archaeology) that is reported in the formal literature goes to great lengths to present another science: universal, context-free and "objective" because the people are systematically removed. Monographs and site reports regularly distort and obscure the organization of knowledge construction (Gilbert and Mulkay 1984). We notice, for instance, that archaeological reports will regularly ignore or invert temporal sequences as though we already knew at the beginning what we actually only learned by the end. Archaeologists will summarize a generalized methodology that is presumed to have been in use for the entire operation when, in fact, changes in procedures are almost always introduced during the course of work for many practical reasons, including that we learn more as we go and our early procedures seem clumsy or unnecessary. We also run out of materials, run out of time, find ways to use team members efficiently even if it violates strict procedure. We make practical on-the-spot revisions when we need to.

But our conventional reports omit this. They omit the negotiations about what *counts* as an adequate record of what was observed, or what counts as "the same thing," or what counts as "agreement." They omit names of crew members, emotions, emergencies, weather, beauty, luck (good or bad) and a host of other circumstances because archaeology as a science relies on the belief that anyone excavating a given location would make the same observations and discoveries, and that the experience of a specific excavation is therefore largely irrelevant. The orthodox scientific report is impoverished by these rules and conventions when context is absent and people have no place.

At Yutopian, I tried to be alert to ways that our conventional archaeological practices constituted a research environment or "context" that in turn conditioned what we "found." I wanted to observe how archaeologists and archaeological practice embodied and reproduced in our everyday work activities, and especially in our decision chains, some aspects of "external" values that ultimately were shaping our results. At the scale I imagined this transpiring, I couldn't record it. I couldn't video the embedded, implicit "background" assumptions and practical skills, the language use and technical know-how that gave form to our interactive work because, as co-director, I was constantly involved in the "foreground": the decision making, planning, assessing and evaluating. The video camera was seldom available even when conscious decisions were being made, and since we conducted business in both Spanish and English, it wasn't always clear to monolingual video assistants when they should be capturing the moment. If filming our sequences failed, other media were needed to highlight this process, and this account partially attempts to do so.

Without delving into the romances and animosities, the body odors, fashion statements and cross-cultural misunderstandings (with generally hilarious but sometimes painful outcomes), I hope you will see the crew (including me) at work here. I will try not to gloss over the messy parts and ambiguous bits (see Bit 3). Without wanting to produce a full-length confessional document, at least I will try not to replicate the sins of my forbearers by making the facts look obvious, unambiguous, transparent and natural. I hope that the constructedness of the information we produced at Yutopian—our very human agency—and the points at which we established and reinforced knowledge structures that we needed will be apparent one way or another in the following pages.

Beyond detailing how we worked, in this account I want to lay out *what we learned* from working at Yutopian. But I must also confess that I'm not always sure about the distinction between what we "learned" and what we should already have known, or actually *did* know! That is, the boundary between what is "known" and what is "new" is neither consistent nor stable since knowledge doesn't circulate uniformly through a population, or even very predictably over time and space. Had we known—or been able to know—all there was about the prehistory of this zone from the eighteenth century on, and been familiar with the work of researchers from different countries (some publishing in languages I can't read), and if I understood in greater depth what there is to understand about clays and plant materials and architectural variants of post and beam construction, et cetera, *and* if I remembered all I had ever read, then perhaps what I claim here as "new" would be less so. That is, what we've learned is clearly and closely related to what we knew when we started, what we should have known, and what we came to realize we knew as we worked. There were things that some of us knew but others learned, and we taught each other.

And there were certainly things that we revealed but never understood because we weren't in a position to learn them or learn from them! As always, ignorance shapes what is known in complex ways, and it is not only and always a passive and monolithic ignorance, but rather a plurality of ignorances: some political and concerned with power relations, some resistant to improvement because of deeply held prejudices and inclinations, some idiosyncratic because of the particularities of the researchers. I feel sure we produced new knowledge working at Yutopian, but the knowledge we produced is conditioned by and reflects what was known previously and most surely is different from what another researcher might have learned by working here.

 3

FRAMEWORK

Ambiguity and the lust for certitude

The second (related) framing concern of this account—which also grows out of feminist issues and practices—is how archaeologists address ambiguity in our work . . . or rather, how we insistently and silently dismiss the high degree of uncertainty that surrounds every phase and feature of archaeological research. The archaeological literature is filled with pronouncements, declarations and assertions of knowledge wrested from archaeological sites without any discussion of the confusion and ambiguity that adheres to many of the facts we recover. Even where we qualify archaeological conclusions by degrees of probability and temper them with calls for more data, it is *certainty* that characterizes how archaeological results are reported in our scholarly work and in the popular press. There is no mention that much archaeological research requires difficult or even impossible interpretive assessments and decisions on the basis of evidence that is incomplete, unfamiliar, indeterminate and/or bewilderingly complex: whether we can detect soil color changes all the way across a profile, whether "this" is a tool, whether various artifacts are "associated" or various events related, et cetera. Animated discussions and anxious deliberations over such matters evaporate in our final accounts and the evidence for the losing side is never seen again.

At Yutopian and in this account I embrace ambiguity, not just as good feminist practice but also as a call for greater responsibility in archaeology. Feminism has generally aligned itself on the side of greater reflexivity in knowledge production, encouraging self-awareness both about how we reach conclusions and about the broader relations between knowledge and knowledge makers (Gero 2007). The acceptance and preservation of ambiguous archaeological evidence also strengthens a central tenet of feminist practice in archaeology: to work toward an archaeology that *interrogates* the past (and more generally challenges the singularity of the real) instead of advancing conclusions as exclusively and exhaustively final and correct (e.g., Conkey and Gero 1991; Kus 2006). That the taming, ignoring, erasing and redefining of ambiguity is contradictory to the long-term interests of accumulating accurate information about the past should become clear in the course of this book. I will urge that we resist imposing meaning on the past—meaning that is modern, disciplinary, homogenizing and universalist—and move instead toward honoring (instead of erasing) the evidence that will not yield to closure.

Much of the ambiguity we confront in archaeology emerges from the data that are frequently incomplete or partial ("indeterminate"), but also stand a good chance of being highly complex, where different interpretive factors are all simultaneously relevant to the same interpretive problem. Issues of "interpretive complexity" require that the related pieces of evidence each be well understood, plus we need to understand how these parts might be interacting, compounded by the fact that we don't always know the nature or degree of relationship between parts. We also recognize that the evidence usually does not determine one unique interpretive or explanatory conclusion and preclude all other alternatives ("under-determination"); there is simply an absence of deciding factors that allow us to choose among other plausible determinations. Issues of under-determination can introduce ambiguity at every level of archaeological understanding, from large explanatory frameworks (characterizations of specific archaeological "cultures" or matters of causation) to chronological and classificatory relationships ("Is this a slightly atypical Condorhuasi sherd?"). Longer discussions of each type of ambiguity are offered in Gero (2007).

In addition to these ontological sources of ambiguity—that is, where the ambiguity lies within the evidence itself—there are many *epistemological* issues that resist certitude, issues that arise from what archaeologists themselves bring to their studies: community values, limits of our experience or our judgments or our imaginations, inconsistencies among researchers or within the same researcher over time, and so on. But I want to focus on one central epistemological issue that we might be able to do something about, an issue I call "the reductionist starting principle."

In seeking unambiguous "facts" in archaeology, we frequently adopt simplified and simplifying assumptions about the pasts we are reconstructing. For instance, we use simplifying assumptions about time and simultaneity, about what is to count as "contemporaneous" in archaeological time. We construct a flattened time frame in archaeology (a house "occupation" or a ceramic "period") that has little to do with how life is lived in the real world, as continuous and fluid, always actively stringing together events over space. We assume all the houses in a village were simultaneously occupied. An activity area of ceramic production gains stability and immobility for hundreds of years. "Populations" of people are motivated for all time by similar values and respond in similar ways to timeless stimuli; all females are women and all males men. We have come to settle for definitions and descriptions of social realities in the past that are flat and dead, bearing little resemblance to the complicated, shifting and nuanced realities featured in ethnographic and other social accounts.

The case against reductionist starting principles can be made another way. Contemporary research into social (or political or economic) issues allows social scientists access to "all" the data, and problems of underdetermination and indeterminacy are supposedly foreclosed because research subjects are fully observable, recordable and open to questioning or inspection by different and complementary modes. Yet researchers of the modern world still can't decide what causes a recession or why the Taliban proves popular. Resolutions to questions posed today are *also* ambiguous because social realities are complex, multicausal, interdeterminant and multivocal, changing from each person's perspective.

Ultimately, we must confront the profound discrepancy between the complicated social realities that we inhabit every day and the flattened, disarticulated, unidimensional and, yes, *unambiguous* social realities that we depict and justify in archaeological pronouncements. What kind of social reality do we think we're describing in the reductionist, oversimplified reconstructions we offer about the past? Or is this just a disciplinary-wide, taken-for-granted wink at a social reality that could not have possibly existed in these simplistic terms but is the best we can manage? Or are we saying prehistoric human systems were actually structured along such lines, effectively denying that human societies and relationships had the same degree of complexity in the past as they do today?

Like simplifying our starting assumptions, archaeologists use other conventionalized practices that stabilize evidence and interpretation, and produce less ambiguous knowledge. I call these practices "mechanisms of closure," including the four listed here:

- *Cleaning the data*: This first strategy is a broad and inclusive set of practices that reduce ambiguity by dampening variance within data and making data sets seem homogeneous. In many instances, "cleaning up data" is classification; it involves using a limited set of semantically broad but conceptually limiting categories into which all evidence is accommodated (band/tribe/chiefdom/state, or tool /utilized flake/debitage). Once grouped semantically (classified), individual pieces of evidence are imbued with stability and similitude by the assumption that evidential classes contain homogeneous materials and, more significantly, homogeneous meanings hold across different times and contexts. Once a data class is defined as an entity ("kitchen area" or "deteriorating environment" or "European-made object"), items can be inventoried, compared by size, mapped in space, and read as carrying the same meanings (or functions, or causal implications) in comparable contexts. A related form of cleaning data (dampening variance) is to pose dichotomous binary options (A vs. Not-A), effectively removing all nonconforming data from consideration. Cleaning up data may involve concentrating on central tendencies and eliminating or ignoring gradients or outliers; often we draw arbitrary boundaries around what we will consider relevant to a problem at hand as a strategy for reducing complexity. Examples of devices that help clean up the data include using Munsell color charts; drawing trowel lines on profiles or feature outlines to assist in illustration; assigning sites to ecological zones and coloring each zone distinctively on a projected slide; drawing isotherms of median artifact densities; clustering data into evolutionary stages or periods.

- *Pushing the data* is what I call the practice of sequentially building an interpretive assertion by first drawing tentative conclusions and then using one's own tentative conclusions as an authority to firm up these conclusions in a later stage of the interpretation until, in the final summing up, one pronounces one's findings as a secure and unambiguous conclusion. So, "it is possible that" later in the text becomes "most likely, this was" and concludes: "as shown previously, it appears that. . . ."

- *Stretching the data* means finding the general in the specific, or generalizing to make "big claims" from specific cases. A plausible functional or causal relationship in a local context is said to hold widely or to stand for a larger class of interpretations where the same relationship would hold. "Stretching the data" is undertaken at all levels of archaeological practice: in abstracting and generalizing stratigraphy to larger regional areas in the form of "A" and "B" horizons, or in erecting typologies for regions from single sites, or in creating semantic categories for variable features. More significantly, "stretching the data" can include pairing one feature in a local context with a large, widely recognized process, thus "demonstrating" the wider process at the local site.

- *Machining data* involves describing or characterizing data by means of an impersonal, often technologically sophisticated machine, or otherwise observing or measuring data not in cultural context but rather against some universal standard, to give an unambiguous reading on specific variables (density, refractivity, chemical composition, etc.) which then forms the basis of the analysis. These practices eliminate intra- and inter-subject variation in interpretation and reduce ambiguity, while also removing cultural significance.

In the archaeological account that follows, I use some of these strategies myself; after all, I am schooled in the practice of archaeological conventions, in the field and the lab and at my desk. But I believe we can do better (1) at identifying and drawing boundaries around some of the specific difficulties in interpretation that are systematically abused and denied, and (2) at honoring unresolved features of archaeological evidence as worthy enigmas to stimulate the imagination and preserve for the future (rather than disappearing them by ignoring them or incorporating them too readily in modern systems of meaning). I hope I make some progress in the pages that follow.

Project Context

 4

NARRATIVE

Project origins in a British steak dinner

My sabbatical for the academic year 1990–1991 should have passed in the mountains of north-central Peru, extending summer field seasons at and around the site of Queyash Alto into an intensified year-long investigation. Instead, the revolutionary political movement known as Sendero Luminoso had been increasingly active throughout the Peruvian highlands, and both the 1988 excavations and the 1989 laboratory work in the regional museum had been marked by threatening face-to-face encounters, murders of acquaintances and bombs too close to ignore. I ended up in Cambridge, England, writing articles and wondering if I would ever be able to return to Queyash.

Cambridge attracts sabbatical scholars, and among the small fellowship of visiting archaeologists was a charming mid-career Argentine, Gustavo Politis, who was suffering the British cuisine, sorely missing Argentinian meat. On one occasion, we drove out of town to a country inn where Gustavo treated himself to a large British steak, thus improving his mood and prompting him (perhaps) to invite me to come and lecture at the university where he was dean while I might also consider a new field project in Argentina.

And there it was. Four months later I arrived in Buenos Aires and was presented to a potential collaborator for archaeology in the Argentinean Andes: Lic. Cristina Scattolin. Scattolin was an experienced and talented archaeologist from the metropolitan center of La Plata and had been conducting research for 20 years in the mountains of Northwest Argentina. Within weeks we set off to tour that part of the country, focused on one of the heartland regions of Argentine archaeology, the north-south-running Calchaquí Valley, with the regional capital city of Santa María located in its southern section (Fig. 2).

The Calchaquí Valley lies on the eastern side of the Andean cordillera and plays a key role linking the high Andean puna and altiplano along the Chilean border on the west with the lower intermontane valleys of Argentina to the south and east. When the Inka expanded their imperial empire in the fifteenth century, they encountered a series of large fortified settlements forming a chain along the high western margins

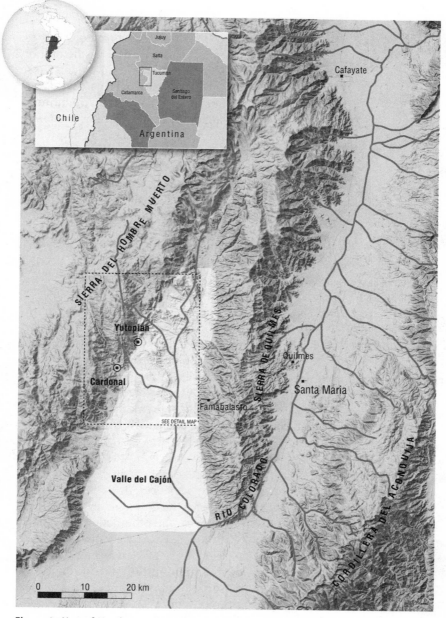

Figure 2. Map of Northwest Argentina (NOA), showing Santa María.

Figure 3. Santamariana burial urn in the form of a woman with cup, from the Museo Provincial Arqueológico "Eric Boman," Santa María (Catamarca), Argentina

of the Calchaquí Valley, built on both sides of the defining Sierra de Quilmes: on the eastern Santa María side and on the western Valle del Cajón side. These were the local Santamariana chiefdoms, and indeed all accounts of Argentinean prehistory feature the famous Santamariana burial urns of the Calchaquí Valley from this era, the Regional Development period (900–1480 CE), just before Inka domination. It was not surprising to find the small regional museum in Santa María offering a fine sample of these impressively large face neck Santamariana pots that sometimes take the form of women's bodies but also feature geometric designs of various sorts (Fig. 3).

But our attention was directed to the earlier prehistory of this zone, an extensive chapter that had received almost no attention since the early years of the twentieth century when proto-archaeologists, travelers and unorthodox scholars had extracted smaller, more finely crafted ceramic vessels from funerary contexts in these areas. Unlike the Santamariana ceramics, the finely polished and modeled grey or black Formative pottery, frequently with incised and punctate markings (Fig. 4), was associated with early settled agricultural life in parts of Northwest Argentina. It was this pattern of Formative life that Scattolin had been focusing on, and that I would join her in studying.

We were fascinated by the possibilities of the Cajón Valley, an enclosed side valley off the Calchaquí that lay just on the other side of the Sierra de Quilmes from Santa María. Scattolin had barely entered the valley previously and recognized it as a region long neglected by archaeologists although research had been conducted there in the mid-1900s (Arena 1975; Cigliano 1958, 1961). At the same time, I was seeking a project area that didn't challenge current projects being undertaken by Argentineans. If my training was in the imperialist tradition of Americans working abroad, then at least I didn't want to overlap with or intrude on research conducted by contemporary Argentinean scholars. Moreover, I am drawn to working in circumscribed regions where prehistoric processes can be studied in a naturally bounded research area and was pleased that the Cajón was delineated by mountain ranges on three sides

Figure 4. Formative period (Candelaria) incised ceramics. Photographs by Martin Franken (VC 9207 and VC 8555) and Claudia Obrocki (VC 6501 and V C 1641), reproduced with kind permission of the Staatliche Museen zu Berlin, Ethnologisches Museum.

(Fig. 5). Although it lacked all amenities like paved roads, electricity and modern facilities, it was also only three or four hours by pickup truck from Santa María. Its Formative period was an inviting empty book.

By the end of our 1991 tour Christina and I were discussing co-directing a new project in the Valle del Cajón. She would bring local

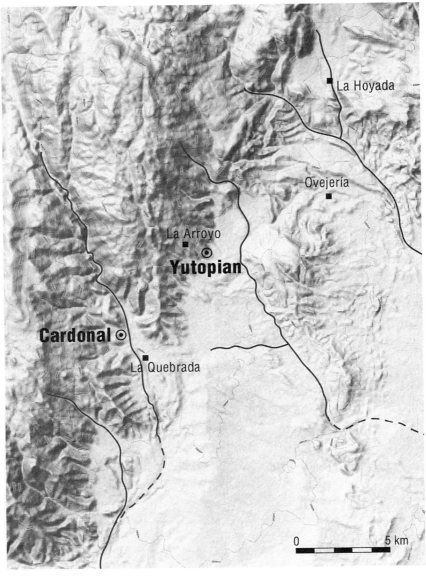

Figure 5. Map of the Valle del Cajón.

knowledge, experience and an adventuresome intellect to the project, plus help with bureaucratic arrangements, and I would try to organize some funding and bring new ideas about gender to the archaeology of Northwest Argentina. Our students would work together in a rich intercultural mix, and together we would forge new methodologies and theoretical perspectives. I also believe we both thought we might enjoy working together.

 # 5

SOCIO-POLITICS

Finding Northwest Argentina

The bus trip from Buenos Aires into the northwest regions starts by crossing the low flat pampas with grazing cows and soybean fields, then climbing through the drizzly rain forest of the eastern Andean slopes with a bus change in the industrial city of San Miguel de Tucumán. From there a regional bus drives due west through the tourist town of Tafí del Valle, climbs up and over the far lip of that valley which divides the Province of Tucumán from the Province of Catamarca, and descends into the lovely southern portion of the Calchaquí Valley (Fig. 6). The remarkable mineral-loaded mountains banded in deep purple, green and red flank the road heading south into Santa María, the small-town capital of the Department of Santa María. With luck, the 1260-km trip from Buenos Aires has taken just under 20 (sleepless) hours.

In Argentina, the northwest region is often referred to as NOA; it includes the treeless altiplano or puna lands on the west, and the *yungas* (jungles) (*selvas occidentales*) on the east, with the *valliserrana* (valley/ mountain zone) in between. Remote from the bustle of Buenos Aires, life in the northwest region is slow paced and not what Argentina's recent President Menem had in mind when he called his country "a first world nation in a third world continent."

In 1991, 1993 and 1994 the town of Santa María occupied only a few blocks of low buildings built around the central plaza with its elegant old trees painted white at their bases. Here in the shadow of the dramatic Sierra de Quilmes to the west, and heated by the bright mountain sun at

Figure 6. Calchaquí Mountains from Caspischango, overlooking the Santa María Valley.

1900 m above sea level, the unrushed people of the town would congregate on benches and eat ice cream, or stroll around the statue of stern General Belgrano that dominates the plaza's intersecting diagonal walkways. There was a Hotel Turista in Santa María but a couple of homes (*residenciales*) also offered rooms to travelers and didn't seem to mind the hefty trunks and overstuffed backpacks that archaeological teams stashed while they shopped and made field arrangements in town.

But more recently we have witnessed Santa María's rapacious growth, in tandem with the development of the Bajo La Alumbrera sluice mine that opened in 1995 about 30 km southeast of Santa María. With the mine in operation, Santa María now bustles with new enterprises and money. Bajo La Alumbrera is the largest gold mine in South America, controlled by Canadian and Australian multinational corporations and seeking to remove as much as 85,000 tons of crude per day. As the rich deposits of gold and copper—mixed with silver, zinc and lead—are drawn up, washed and slushed overland to Tucumán 65 km to the east, new restaurants, hotels, nightclubs and housing blocks have sprung up in large developments; now there are several traffic lights and three car dealerships. No matter that this environment is a fragile high desert, receiving only a few inches of rain a year. The water table is conveniently plumbed, and many local people who practiced subsistence agriculture only a few years ago now rotate working at the mines for shifts of twelve days on, four days off. These workers are not the patrons of the new restaurants, hotels and car dealerships in town; it is the engineers and managers from other large cities who support the new enterprises, often buying homes in this attractive region where there is sun 365 days a year, as the pamphlets remind us.

We archaeologists (the Yutopian project is among several that operate out of Santa María) find this burgeoning development both irritating and facilitating. New hardware stores, copy centers and office supply stores undoubtedly make it easier to locate and replace necessities for the field. Finding hot water at the end of a busy day is also much appreciated. The archaeology museum "Eric Boman" has moved to a prominent location on the plaza and is spruced up to attract visitors, partly with our well-labeled exhibitions about Yutopian. Still, the traditional Andean flavor of old Santa María is palpable, with horses being ridden into town on market days and homespun clothing frequently in evidence.

Ironically, when archaeologists are in town we look like the mine managers in our dress and physical appearance: we're too tall and too light-skinned to be locals. We too wave our government permits that legitimate what we do here (plumb the earth for its treasures); we also have goals that align with interests outside the local region rather than in it. We like to think we treat people well and that we make significant contributions to the Santa María schools and museum (see Bit 70), but when an agenda is set many miles away, and when that agenda has consequences for the local people who have had little to do with establishing or implementing it, it is always, arguably, a form of imperialism (see Bit 10).

After we have made our purchases and photocopied our field forms, checked in with local authorities and made last phone calls, we are ready to head off to Yutopian. During the first years of the project our transportation into the field from Santa María depended on tracking down Señor Beto Llampa who might be anywhere in town. Importantly, he owned and drove a pickup truck regularly into the Valle del Cajón west of Santa María to ferry people and goods back and forth. He told us only that he had relatives in one of the valley communities, but later we figured out that he had grown up in the Cajón and, like many others, had abandoned his land and farming to do construction work in Santa María. (Now, of course, Don Beto works in the new mine, and we have had to rely on the municipality for travel to the field.) For $100 he would pile all of us and our gear, food and supplies into the pickup and head south on Route 40, the famous north-south highway through western Argentina from the Bolivian border down to Patagonia.

For the first 45 minutes out of Santa María, the road to Yutopian follows the base of the Sierra de Quilmes and the course of the Río Colorado

Figure 7.
View of the
Valle del
Cajón (look-
ing east).

which flows at its feet, going through small villages with colorful names like Palo Seco (Dry Stick), Loro Huasi (Parrot Home) and Casa de Piedra (Stone House). But at the southern terminus of the Quilmes range we leave Route 40 as the river and our new road make a dramatic hairpin twist around the base of the mountain and head northward, entering the pocket-shaped side valley known as the Valle del Cajón (*cajón* means "drawer"). On dusty roads we follow the river north toward its source at the constricted head of the valley 90 km away (Fig. 7), bumping over rises and dips, through threatening patches of sand strewn with cactus wood to ease the passage. Occasionally we pass an isolated adobe house with adjacent corrals, or a few free-ranging goats or cattle, or a rare llama in the dry scrub chaparral landscape. On one trip, Don Beto pulled off the dirt road and unloaded some plastic sacks and cardboard boxes next to a big tree with no buildings or people in sight—and drove off. "They expect this delivery and will come by tonight," he told us, but we couldn't imagine who that would be or where they would come from.

With luck it takes three hours to the center of the valley where we abruptly turn left at a marker that is invisible to us city dwellers and head west across the valley, sometimes driving in the riverbed and sometimes through steep bedrock formations until we reach the mountains that define the far western margin of the valley, the Sierra del Hombre Muerto (Dead Man Mountains). There we climb more slowly up onto the lower slopes as the road gets less and less traveled toward Yutopian. Gaining elevation, we can see the Valle del Cajón spread out below: a flat expanse of dry uplands dotted with saguaro cacti and boulder outcroppings. The steeply defined mountains that enclose the valley on the east (Sierra de Quilmes) are often visible from the western margins since the valley is only 20 km wide at this point. Because we are usually there during the Argentinean winter (summer in North America), there is often a dusting of snow on the highest peaks (see Fig. 6). The few homesteads we can spot are marked by plantings of *álamos* (poplar trees), visual clues to habitations in an otherwise treeless landscape.

What is striking overall is the absence of villages or even homesteads here, the extremely low population density, while the nearby Calchaquí Valley has strings of villages along the roads and many towns between them. Cristina tells me that the Valle del Cajón was known in earlier decades of the twentieth century as a prosperous region with a healthy population and strong agricultural production. It was also known for its Peronista political sympathies, and when Juan Perón was ousted in 1955, the new "Radical" government refused to make improvements or provide resources to the area. This bit of apocrypha may only partially explain why neither electricity nor telephones have ever been installed here even though they are commonplace and long in use elsewhere; in the Cajón there are no paved roads and no jobs, and the population is dwindling. In the 12 years we worked there, I personally knew 14 people who died or moved away, and I knew of no new families who moved in. Most people who live in Santa María have never been in this valley although it lies just on the other side of the Quilmes range which they look at every day and treat as a boundary to their known universe.

Facts

- The Cajón is 90 km long and 30 km wide at the southern entrance.
- Pico Colorado, the highest peak in Sierra del Hombre Muerto, reaches 4450 masl.
- Cerro Negro, the highest peak in Sierra de Quilmes, reaches 4720 masl.
- Average annual rainfall is approximately 250 mm/year, mostly in summer.

6

NARRATIVE

Archaeologists and *lugareños* meet at Yutopian

In the North American summer of 1993, after university classes had ended and last grades were passed in, I went off to survey the Valle del Cajón for Formative sites. I had secured five weeks of grant money for Cristina Scattolin and myself but at the last minute Cristina had to stay in La Plata with family health issues; I would have to go up to Northwest Argentina alone and find another companion. On top of that, the July weather at 3000 m above sea level was colder than usual and very much colder than the South Carolina summer I had just left. I was able to convince a University of Catamarca archaeology student to accompany me, a young man with a sullen, provincial swagger whose eagerness to earn a salary and gain archaeological experience in an unknown region was barely greater than his reluctance to take orders from a foreigner—and a female at that. Prospects seemed bleak.

We arranged with Don Beto for a ride to a central point in the Cajón, the community of La Hoyada with its regional school (grades 1–9), a dozen adobe houses, a well-maintained soccer pitch, and assorted noisy animals including, critically, several mules that were quickly enlisted for transport (Fig. 8). With the school custodian Tango as guide, we made our way through the valley from one isolated homestead to another, staying with local families and asking about archaeological sites. The modern settlement pattern conformed closely to our model of Formative life: extended families dispersed across the landscape, each maintaining its own field systems and corrals, while homesteads were composed of single-room structures arranged around a central open patio where a wide range of domestic and agricultural tasks were undertaken (Fig. 9). But the archaeological sites we encountered did not conform to this pattern and were clearly not Formative; they were large with extensive and densely packed architectural remains, littered with the well-known Santamariana painted ceramics of the Regional Development period. We encountered none of the polished grey or black ceramics or the incised or punctate sherds that would correspond to earlier occupations.

Figure 8. Preparing the mules at La Hoyada for survey.

Figure 9. Contemporary homestead in the Valle del Cajón, similar to Early Formative cluster of structures around an open patio.

By the end of two weeks we were dirty and discouraged, and my Argentinean companion had had just about enough of traveling with a demanding gringa boss who insisted on starting work at 8:30 a.m. and eating sandwiches instead of a proper cooked midday meal. We had traveled widely, on foot and on animals, and only the extreme western margins of the valley were left to explore. It was unclear whether it would be worth the effort to get there given how tired we were, how unsure the route, and how absent Formative sites seem to be in this valley.

But leaving the valley wasn't easy either. And the family at La Ovejería, the last homestead we visited, was especially kind and encouraging (and prosperous), showering us with hospitality, taking time to show us an Inka site on the edge of their terrain, cooking us hot meals and letting us sleep in the warmest part of their house. Also, the next day they expected a party of neighbors—pilgrims!—to pass through their *rancho* en route to the very area we wanted to visit on the western flanks of the valley, and surely the group would be pleased to take us with them. My disgruntled student wasn't convinced, and I was getting sick with a stuffy head and pounding headache that didn't go away no matter what I drank, ate or swallowed. We vacillated. This last opportunity to access the isolated western valley margins would also take us farther from the only routes out of the valley. The grumpy student muttered and kicked dust around with his boots.

The following day was bright and sunny, and the expected group arrived at La Ovejería, having walked 45 km down to Route 40 and 45 km back, carrying a wooden litter with a boxed image of San Juan on various stalwart shoulders. They had attended the festival at Cerro Colorado where San Juan, patron saint of the valley, had been blessed by the itinerant priest, and they had conducted some trading as well. Everyone had been drinking and now had to share more sustenance and drink with the Pachao family before they set off again on the final 12 km of their journey. We were introduced and they agreed to take us west with them. We could stay with the man called Jorge Chaile, a handsome farmer about 40 years old who was one of the image bearers (Fig. 10). Jorge removed his black fedora and held it in front of his chest, bowed a tipsy little bow, and assured us (if we understood him correctly) that his very modest home was ours if we wished to stay there as long as we understood that it was very *humilde* (humble). I protested mildly, feeling pretty awful and unfit for travel, but when our host saddled a horse for me and I was too ambivalent to argue, my fate was sealed. Never mind that the journey seemed wildly improbable. "How would I be able to return the horse?" I asked. Don Roque was unconcerned: I had only to unsaddle her at Jorge's place, remove her bridle, slap her on the rump and she would come home! There was nothing more to say.

Figure 10. Jorge Chaile with his family's image of San Juan.

We set off then, our procession, winding our way through the empty hills, filling them with plaintive music, a bright sinuous line of color and sound against the muted earth tones and the otherwise complete silence of the winter landscape. We were 14 people all told, some on foot and others on horseback or mule, led by a flag-waving patriot and fol-

Figure 11. The pilgrims' procession toward Yutopian.

lowed by two other banner carriers, two drum players, several flautists and an accordion player(!), plus a grandmother riding side-saddle on a mule, another grandmother walking firmly, a passel of children and several pack mules. Flags unfurled, San Juan in his box hoisted high, the music in full tilt under the midday sun, we filled the landscape and multiplied our numbers with sound and motion so that our small group was almost a crowd and couldn't be swallowed by the landscape. I was feverish on my swaying horse and managed to take only a few wobbly, out-of-focus photos as we moved through the motionless landscape (Fig. 11), entrusted entirely to our guides who sang, banged and blew their way west, carrying their blessed saint home. Forty-five minutes from Jorge's residence we stopped and Jorge lit a contained brush fire to signal ahead that we were on our way, and I rested gratefully on the ground a few moments.

In the last rays of daylight when our destination finally came into view, it was hard to make it out; the long adobe house and the linear hill behind it were made of the same soft brown earth. The four side-by-side rooms of the house opened in the same direction onto a narrow terrace that served as a common activity area. Other terraces fell from the house to the fields below and also rose up behind it, but lest the house disappear entirely into the landscape, several old *álamo* trees rose in sharp peaks around it, marking this location from the vast space around it. Smoke rose from the central kitchen room with sweet cooking aromas greeting us amid calls of welcome and grand gestures of flinging down burdens and gear. We were invited to a beautifully laid table to celebrate the homecoming of the now-blessed saint.

But this was not for me: this food, this chatter, this animation. I asked whether I could lie down anywhere; my head was throbbing and I was alternately shivering and perspiring. Jorge took me to the last room at the end of the house, a storage room where a straw bed was quickly made up for me with sheets and heavy home-woven blankets. San Juan himself was housed here, together with the musical instruments, various changes of clothes and a heap of agricultural tools. I fell on the bed greedily, not bothering to take off my shoes. All my joints were aching, my head felt like it would explode and I closed my eyes as if forever.

Sometime later Jorge returned, accompanied by his sister Ramona (the cook of the feast) to look in on me. "Would you like to be cured?" they asked. I didn't hesitate: "Yes, thank you," I snuffled, hot and shivering, I certainly did want to be cured. So Jorge and Ramona set about the task: they noted my fever and explained that was why my feet were cold. They took off my shoes and rubbed my feet wonderfully with something that felt cool, wet and divine; they rubbed my hands and reached down into my sweater to rub my shoulders as well. Then they offered me a warm infusion that smelled of flowers and sweet herbs which I drank slowly and gratefully, and then they covered my head with a sheet, speaking chants or prayers that I couldn't understand. They sat with me in silence. Then Jorge briefly took my hands, and when I started to cry, surely from the fever and the relief of lying down, Jorge pronounced that it seemed I was sick because of a recent death of a loved one. Taken aback, I snuffled and cried some more, thinking of my recently deceased mother, and then I fell asleep to the distant noises of laughter and singing and eating, a candle still burning in front of the newly returned saint.

I awoke 36 hours later when the Catamarca student burst into my room. His happiness was uncontained: on the ridgetop behind the house was an extensive Formative site with terraced levels carved into its northern and eastern faces and covered with sherds of burnished grey and burnished black pottery, some incised and some punctated, as well as the preserved foundations of stone houses. Indeed, the sherds he was holding were exactly what we'd been searching for, and within hours I was up on the ridgetop myself, verifying that the site promised everything we had been looking for to investigate Formative lifestyles, but larger and more elaborate than the regional Formative sites we knew. Surface materials included a piece of hammered bronze, lithic debris of an unusual variety of raw materials, several figurines—and from the highest point, a view across the entire Cajón Valley (Fig. 12). I asked Jorge what he called this ridge, this unexpected new archaeological place with so much promise, and he told us "Yutopian." I just had to laugh out loud with the rightness of it all: a most excellent Formative site delivered up by a saint and called by a name which in Quechua means something about a hill full of partridges but that sounded to my English-trained ears precisely like the word UTOPIA!!!!

That Catamarca student never worked with our project again. But we worked at Yutopian in 1994, 1996 and 1998, conducted an analysis

Figure 12. Yutopian ridge with the Chaile homestead on the right and walled gardens in the center.

season in Santa María in 1999, and worked at nearby Formative Cardonal in 2004. Through these years, many archaeologists and students of archaeology from Argentina and the United States would come to know and respect, depend on and admire Jorge Chaile and his family (Fig. 13). When we returned the following year, in 1994, Jorge's mother had passed away at what was believed to be age 91. Jorge, a bachelor, had by then built himself a two-room adobe house some 40 m above his family's old homestead and had moved the image of San Juan up the hill with him. Down below in the old house, his adoptive sister Ramona still lived with her three young children. Two of Jorge's uncles, Federico (58 years old) and Álvaro (45), were also unmarried and each lived by himself within a 10– to 15-minute walk from Jorge's house in different directions. Jorge's birth sister Celia lived with her husband Nicholas Araoz ("El Blanquito") and their three girls 4 km away in a location they called Lagunita, or Little Lake, which we could just make out from the height of Yutopian. Jorge's aunt Elisa lived with her husband Cleto 2 km in the other direction, at La Arroyo, where they ran a tiny store in one of their outbuildings, our major source of matches, noodles, candles, soap powder and locally produced red wine. Much later, we learned that Jorge had two other aunts who also lived within a radius of 10 km from him.

By the last time we visited Yutopian in 2004, Jorge had married Santo, the eldest daughter of Don Roque Pachao from La Ovejería,

Figure 13. Jorge Chaile and family in 1993.

perhaps because he had saved enough money and gained enough status by working with our project to now be considered properly eligible. They do not have children. Jorge has continued his weaving, together with keeping his free-ranging chickens, goats and cows, planting and harvesting a wide range of edible crops, and building several more outbuildings at Yutopian above the old homestead. Although he owns a new gas stove, stored carefully in an adobe room in its original plastic, he and Santo continue to cook outside over fires on the patio in front of the house. There is a new rabbit hutch and the beginning of a workshop building for weaving. The old homestead below stands empty, and the thatched roof has caved in irreparably.

Ramona now has five children and has moved to San José, near Santa María, because the large old house was too hard to keep up by herself. Her oldest daughter, Jenny, whom we first met when she was seven, is now a mother herself. Neither Federico nor Álvaro has married, although Álvaro had a visiting girlfriend for several years (the cook at the regional school in La Quebrada, 8 km to the south). Celia's husband Nicholas now works in town regularly and visits the Cajón only on weekends; their oldest and most capable daughter María Louisa has also moved to San José to attend high school, interrupted briefly by the birth of her first child.

Facts

- In 1994–1999 the population at Yutopian was eight, plus five at Lagunita.
- In 2004 the population at Yutopian was three, plus three at Lagunita.
- Elevation of site: 3200 masl.
- Yutopian ridgetop: 330 m long (N-S) and 100 m across (E-W).

7

BACKSTORY

Chronology in Northwest Argentina

In the late nineteenth and early twentieth centuries impressive collections of beautifully made ceramics, elaborate bronze pieces, stone masks and other archaeological treasures were amassed without science or ceremony from Northwest Argentina (Fig. 14) and sold to museums across Europe and the Americas. It wasn't until the mid-twentieth century however that scholars began to propose chronological frameworks for understanding these objects and the cultures that produced them (Bennett et al. 1948; Cigliano 1958, 1961; González 1955, 1963;

Figure 14. Manuel Zavaleta (right) overseeing excavation of Santamariana burial urns, ca. 1900. Photograph from Zavaleta 1906: 298.

González and Cowgill 1975; González and Núñez Regueiro 1962). Rex González's scheme for subdividing prehistoric time was based on a taxonomy of chronologically significant, commonly used ceramic styles (beginning with a Preceramic period). An alternative, explicitly Marxist system of periodization was put forward based on contrastive modes of production (Núñez Regueiro 1974, 1978) or on adaptive phases (Olivera 1987, 2001), beginning with a "predatory" or pre-agricultural phase (hunters and gatherers) and essentially representing evolutionary stages of human adaptation. Over time and with the accumulation of ^{14}C dates, a broad outline of prehistoric social change across Northwest Argentina has solidified, although nomenclature and dates still vary from author to author and valley to valley (cf. Leoni and Acuto 2008; Tarragó 2000); in a generalized fashion it looks something like this (loosely following Johansson 1996:63):

- Archaic period (1000–200 BCE), characterized by a hunting and gathering way of life, with cultivation gradually playing an increasing role in the economy;
- Formative period (200 BCE–900 CE), associated with the practice of agriculture and village life, with marked regionalization. This period is frequently subdivided into an Early Formative (200 BCE–500 CE) and a Late Formative (500 CE–900 CE);
- Regional Development period (900 CE–1480 CE), when ranked or stratified societies appeared, eventually to be conquered by the Inka.

Not surprisingly, the archaeology of the Regional Development period (RDP) is the most prominent and best-documented cultural time period in the Santa María Valley as a result of its rich material past and many decades of survey and excavation, but also from the ample discussion and debate about the justly famous RDP Santamariana funerary urns displayed in provincial museums throughout Northwest Argentina (Fig. 15). In fact, RDP sites produced a large proportion of the massive nineteenth-century collections, and Santamariana was the first archaeological style to be identified and named (Lafone Quevedo 1892, cited in Nastri 2008:9).

RDP sites are recognized as large population agglomerations covering extensive areas of housing that consist of irregularly agglutinated structures. Houses are spacious and apparently accommodated extended groups or families; storage facilities are typically located within the domestic structures. Populations are supported by extensive terraced agricultural zones of maize, some irrigated. Cemeteries with infant burials in huge ceramic urns are common, and adults are interred in cyst graves (Ottonello and Lorandi 1987:82).

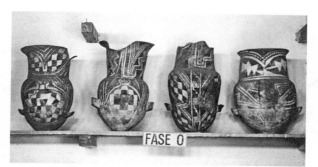

Figure 15. Santa-mariana urns in the Museo Provincial Arqueológico "Eric Boman," Santa María.

Figure 16. Quilmes, a reconstructed Regional Development period site in the Santa María Valley.

In the Santa María Valley, RDP residential sites often occupy extensive areas on the flanks of hills while the hilltops themselves are fortified. A series of such RDP hill town/forts is located along the eastern flanks of the Sierra del Cajón at approximate 10-km intervals.[1] Quilmes, one of the best-known and earliest excavated of these, is clearly composed of distinct sectors: a protected slope of enclosed structures on the upper hillside and, at some distance, a densely populated village with its own water reserves. The site of Quilmes has been reconstructed in recent times and is an important tourist destination today (Fig. 16). Two other RDP sites in the Santa María Valley have been studied in long-term, ongoing research projects that have yielded especially valuable information: Rincón Chico, studied by Myriam Tarragó and her team from the Museo Etnográfico in Buenos Aires, and El Pichao, studied by a Swedish project from the University of Göteborg under the overall direction of Per Cornell.

RDP ceramics are typically painted, often employing black and red designs on a white painted surface (Santamariana tricolor), or using black designs on a white surface (bicolor), or less often black designs on a red surface. In fact, surface collections from RDP sites show painted ceramics outnumbering plainwares (Nastri 2008:12). Large open bowls and pots are common, but scholars of Santamariana ceramics focus on the highly decorated funerary urns produced not only in RDP times but throughout the Inka (1480–1536) and early Colonial (1536–1650) periods. Often the urn is used with a shallow bowl inverted over its opening. Urns vary in overall size, sometimes reaching a height of 65 cm, but proportions of vessel bodies and vessel necks also vary, as do the design fields and designs. Various typologies are argued; major groupings of distinctive urns have been recognized by region, each named for the area where it was first encountered: San José (generally considered the earliest type), Santa María, Belén and Famabalasto (Johansson 1996; see also Weber 1978, 1981). A six-phase typology has been constructed specifically for the urns of the Santa María Valley by Podestá and Perrota (1973; Perrota and Podestá 1978) and is still used today (Nastri 2008); this sequence suggests the evolution of an increasingly human form, first female (Weber 1981) but giving way to more masculine forms until in the last phase urn designs become highly abstracted (Fig. 17). The projectile points of this period are small, stemless, triangular points attached to arrow shafts and mobilized with bows.

When we turn to the earlier Formative period, and especially in the Santa María Valley, the research is significantly less well developed (Scattolin 2007; Tarragó and Scattolin 1999). An Early and a Late Formative period (also called Lower and Upper Formative) are distinguished, defined on the basis of distinct ceramic styles and supported with [14]C

Figure 17. Drawing of Santamariana urn sequence (after Nastri 2008: Figure 5; and Perrota and Podestá 1978: Figures 5, 6).

| Phase 0 | Phase 1 | Phase 2 | Phase 3 | Phase 4 | Phase 5 |

dates. But conceptually the Early Formative has largely served as a place-holder in a grand evolutionary scheme, a developmental stage parallel to the European Neolithic and associated with the adoption of an agro-pastoral lifestyle along with the tools that make that lifestyle possible: ceramics, weaving and permanent settlements (Tarragó 2000:302). Early Formative people are portrayed as having lived in egalitarian societies exhibiting little social differentiation and organized by kinship along the lines of simple tribal societies (Raffino 1991; Tarragó 1980); their dispersed residences appear to have grown by replication and fission in relation to available lands to provide access to resources and exchange networks (Tarragó 2000:307). In contrast Núñez Regueiro (1999; Tartusi and Núñez Regueiro 2001) characterizes the Early Formative as evidencing some degree of ranking, arguing that a special-function ceremonial center exists at Alamito (Tartusi and Núñez Regueiro 2001).

Under either argument, most of the Early Formative population is held to have lived in dispersed, low-density distributions across the landscape, conforming to different settlement formations. In much of the region, but especially in the central dry *valliserrana* (valley-mountain) area where Santa María and Yutopian are situated, isolated homesteads are composed of two or three agglutinated structures surrounded by agricultural fields and corrals, sometimes terraced to conform to the surrounding gradients (Tarragó 2000:308) (Fig. 18). Alternatively, residences may consist of circular dry-stone walled habitations arranged around a central circular patio, as in the Tafí Valley east of Yutopian (Berberián 1989).

In addition to the Early Formative settlements in the *valliserrana* zone (including Condorhuasi, Ciénaga and Saujil), Early Formative set-

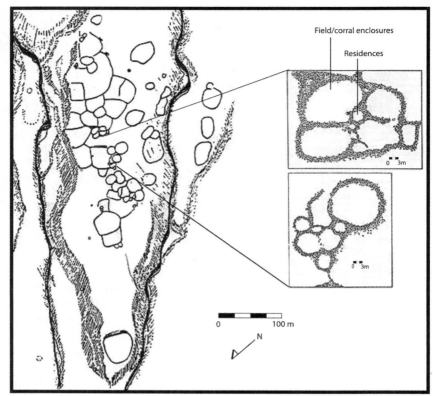

Figure 18. Loma Alto: Individual homesteads surrounded by field and corral enclosures, characteristic of dispersed Early Formative settlements (after Scattolin 1990: Figure 5).

tlements are known from the *quebradas* that connect with the upland puna zone (Alfarcito, Las Cuevas, Campo Colorado) and from the puna itself (Tebenquiche, Laguna Blanca), as well as from the lower *selvas occidentales* (Candelaria) (Ottonello and Lorandi 1987:67–68). By 500 CE villages—and a village way of life—had emerged widely, evidenced in some places by large mounds of successive occupations.

The ceramic styles identified with the Early Formative period vary by region rather than composing a solid chronological sequence. In the central *valliserrana* zone, the most widely recognized Early Formative ceramic styles include the temporally overlapping Candelaria, Condorhuasi, Río Diablo and Vaquerías, with Ciénaga extending somewhat longer in time (Figs. 19 and 20). Many of these styles are defined with subphases or variants (Tartusi and Núñez Regueiro 2001) and some examples rival the finest pottery made anywhere in the Andes.² Early Formative vessels throughout Northwest Argentina (and in many parts of the Americas) are burnished or polished, punctated and incised; the use of polished black and polished grey (unpainted) ceramics, and sometimes polished redwares, is widespread. Sometimes Early Formative vessels are slip-painted a single color, red (or on the Candelaria face

Figure 19. Variety of Early Formative ceramic styles (Candelaria, Yokasil and Vaquerías). Photographs by Martin Franken, reproduced with kind permission of the Staatliche Museen zu Berlin, Ethnologisches Museum.

Figure 20. Condorhuasi ceramics from the Museo Provincial Arqueológico "Eric Boman," Santa María.

Figure 21. Early Formative stone sculpture known as a *suplicante*. Photograph courtesy of Cristina Scattolin.

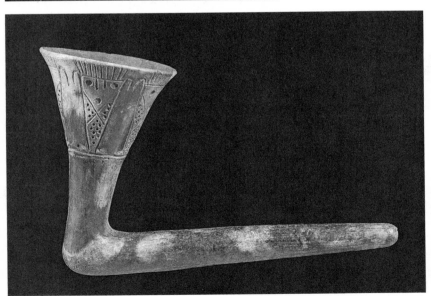

Figure 22. Early Formative pipe. Photograph by Claudia Obrocki, reproduced with kind permission of the Staatliche Museen zu Berlin, Ethnologisches Museum.

neck vessels at Yutopian, white), but the paint is always appl
they are fired (in contrast to the RDP postfire painting of vesse.
the two- and three-color Condorhuasi sherds, highly burnishe
painted, had the color applied before firing.

In addition to ceramics, Early Formative signature materials inclu
elaborate stonework including the iconic sculptures known as *suplı-
cantes* (supplicants) (Fig. 21), stone mortars with complex shapes, and
masks of polished stone. Long ornate tubular pipes (Fig. 22) made in
both stone and ceramic with elaborated modeled, incised or sculpted
bowls occur at all Early Formative sites going back to the earliest, around
600 BCE; these are used "ritually" for smoking hallucinogenic herbs
(Ottonello and Lorandi 1987:70). Alloys of copper were employed by
most Early Formative groups to make decorative ornaments such as
bracelets (see Fig. 1) or small chisels or bells, but Early Formative copper
masks have also been recovered (Scattolin 2006:364, Fig. 7; Scattolin et
al. 2007/2008; Scattolin et al. 2010).

In the chronology of Northwest Argentina, the Early Formative period
ends around 500 CE and is followed by a "lapse" of several hundred
years before the Regional Development period begins in 900 CE. Only
in the *valliserrana* area in central NOA is this lapse accounted for with a
Late Formative (also called the Regional Integration period) associated
with the widespread adoption of Aguada pottery. Known from more than
2000 tombs in the Hualfín Valley (González 2000:288), Aguada refers
to a fine burnished blackware incised within delimited zones, with white
paint filling in the incised lines (Fig. 23). Aguada ceramics show a clear
derivation from late Ciénaga incised pots but are readily recognized for
their shallow bowl forms and figurative decorations including motifs
of felines with *guerreros* (warriors or decapitators) or individuals with
elaborated headdresses or trophy heads. Population growth during this
period may account for why Aguada people were forced to conquer new
agricultural lands, leading to themes of aggression and war (Ottonello
and Lorandi 1987:79).

The conventionalized iconography of Aguada pottery has suggested
a unifying ideology observed throughout the central part of Northwest
Argentina where population growth led to widespread village life. New
indications of high-ranked statuses and increases in ceremonial space
suggest a surge toward complexity (Tarragó 2000:302), and new types
of maize appeared during this time, but in many regards life was still
deeply embedded in Early Formative ways, and a great deal of continuity in lifeways is observed. Pipes continue in use. Both Early and Late
Formative ceramics include undecorated thin-walled polished and burnished grey- and blackware bowls and jars, sometimes with appliqué
rims and even small nubbins or animal head motifs on the rims.

Figure 23. Aguada ceramic from the Museo de La Plata.

This brief outline of NOA chronology and ceramic types requires a confession: other archaeologists working in the region know far more about ceramic types than I do, and it is always impressive to watch groups of young researchers poring over collections and energetically calling out sherd designations, demonstrating their skill at recognizing fine distinctions in what I consider a bewildering array of terms within different systems of nomenclature. I have more to say about this situation in the next Bit.

Notes

1. These and other RDP settlements also contain substantial Inka period and sometimes even later components.

2. Tartusi and Núñez Regueiro (2001) argue that Early Formative contemporaneous "styles" might represent a separation between utilitarian and votive functions.

8

ARGUMENT

Ceramic sequences and social processes

My Argentinean colleagues are adamant, and they are certainly not alone, that ceramic typologies—and the chronologies that can be built from them—lie at the heart of archaeology. No matter that the difficult methodical and technical work required to build a chronological sequence—for a valley or a watershed or a modern political unit—is tedious. The fact is (they say) that whether we ultimately want to reconstruct patterns of social, political or economic life, or understand cognitive processes, risk tolerance or how individuals in the past experienced their lives, we first need control over the chronology so we can "see" what went with what. Only after we assign chronological dates to sites, or to the occupations within sites and to the activities and artifacts within occupations, placing each in its associative chronological position—only then can we determine which activities, occupations and sites are contemporaneous and therefore participated in the same social patterns.

Given the widely accepted view that we must have temporal control before we can learn about social arrangements, it is frustrating that the elaborate, decorated Formative ceramics of Northwest Argentina resist easy temporal ordering. While Rex González and others have taught us how to identify Early Formative versus Late Formative or RDP ceramic styles with relative ease, these still correspond to gross blocks of time of several hundred years each. And despite the elaborate terminology that formalizes sometimes minute differences between Formative ceramic styles, archaeologists have had little success identifying fine-grained sequences of specific attributes within these styles that might correspond to shorter use spans and thus offer more accurate ceramic chronometrics.

This failure of Argentina's ceramics to yield fine-grained chronological sequences is all the more frustrating because such sequences have been worked out successfully in other parts of the Andes. Argentinean Early Formative pottery (200 BCE to 500 CE), for instance, is roughly contemporaneous with Early Intermediate period ("Master Craftsman period") styles of the Peruvian Andes. Like the Argentinean

Condorhuasi and Candelaria styles, the well-known Peruvian Nazca and Moche pots are finely tempered, smoothed and finished, thin-walled and figurative. By many ceramic measures, the Peruvian and Argentinean styles would be considered equally specialized, equally fine, and equally labor intensive: they all require select raw materials and control over technical production details such as sequencing joins of separate clay parts, firing vessels that have parts of different thicknesses, post-firing treatment to obtain smooth finishes, and material know-how to produce a range of paint pigments. It is certain that both sets of ceramics were produced by trained specialists who, in each area, must also have understood the aesthetic conventions and degree of conformity required or permitted. Yet the Peruvian Moche and Nazca styles have been seriated (based on burial lots), so that we can identify early and late variants within each style (Donnan 1978:52–53, after unpublished notes by Larco Hoyle; Proulx 1968, after Rubini and Dawson n.d.), while the Argentinean Early Formative ceramics remain resistant to even the most earnest efforts to produce sequences. Without Early Formative pottery sequences, Argentinean archaeologists are forced to rely on ^{14}C dates to date archaeological components (Bit 71), a requirement that is both expensive and not always possible to fulfill. Archaeologists of the Argentinean Early Formative might legitimately suffer from "Moche envy" in lacking ceramic attributes that collectively and reliably change over time.

But I offer a more optimistic reading of this situation, one that stands the starting assumption on its head and denies that effective chronological sequences must be in place before we can understand social processes. At least some social understandings—specifically about the social, economic and political arrangements of ceramic production—are open to us precisely because the ceramics will not yield to seriation. Let's look back at the Moche (Peruvian) Early Intermediate period ceramics where we know quite a lot about the socio-political arrangements underpinning high-status pottery production. Archaeology done at Moche workshops (e.g., Chapdelaine 2008) and the high degree of iconographic standardization suggest that producers of fine ceramics were almost certainly attached specialists (that is, high-ranking producers who were directly supported by elites in order to fashion high-status pottery). As we understand these arrangements, innovation and change would have been initiated at the top of a hierarchy of producers, and regular stylistic shifts would occur more or less simultaneously over an entire region controlled by the commissioning lord, as his or her specialists incorporated new features into a carefully controlled workshop repertoire.

But how was the elaborate pottery of Northwest Argentina produced? No empirical clues have been produced so far, but everything we know suggests very different socio-political conditions and organizational arrangements, still yielding exquisite, labor-intensive ceramics but without the broadly observed and tightly sequenced stylistic shifts. In NOA, recognized Early Formative styles were produced continuously over a longer sustained period within a distinct region. Thus, traditions of Condorhuasi or Ciénaga pottery most likely correspond to the work of independent specialized ceramicists, perhaps hereditary potters who worked as specialized families or clans, and who continued to make specific kinds or styles of pottery which they provisioned to surrounding populations in some kind of exchange network. Such family-controlled pottery production groups are known today in different parts of Africa (Rod and Susan McIntosh, personal communication), illustrating a set of arrangements where there is little incentive to change styles and more constraints that keep styles (or "types") stable over time. Transgenerational, family-controlled pottery-production "guilds" are only one suggestion for how the regionally based variation in Early Formative ceramics might have been structured, but some such independent production system provides a strong model for understanding the complexity of Early Formative ceramic styles that we observe across Northwest Argentina.

I raise this argument for two reasons. First, it will quickly be seen that in this volume I make little reference to the welter of differentiated ceramic types and subtypes that Argentinean researchers rely upon to describe their materials. I excuse myself partly because in Northwest Argentina, ceramics do not lead to fine-grained chronological understandings in any direct manner. And as I've tried to argue here, even if we did have well-developed ceramic sequences in NOA, these would not necessarily lead to greater understanding of social, political or economic arrangements. In fact just the opposite is true: by understanding social processes we can gain insights into how chronological indicators work (or don't). My other reason for offering this argument is that if we think we have to solve the chronology issues before we can understand social, political and economic arrangements in prehistory, we are doomed to devise ever finer stylistic distinctions, forever naming what we see without seeing what we aim for.

9

NARRATIVE

Why excavate at Yutopian?

Locating Yutopian in 1993 already produced exciting new information about the little-known Early Formative: the site was larger than other regionally known sites of the period and contained clusters of circular enclosures, representing a bigger settlement than the expected dispersed farming homestead (*if* we could be sure they were all Early Formative structures, which we didn't know). It also showed us worked metal on the surface, although again this might belong to a later period given that significant amounts of Santamariana materials were also found on the surface. In any case we could already recognize a wide diversity of Early Formative surface materials with high densities in places, so that even without digging, we could report a substantial Early Formative presence at the location.

Did we have to dig at Yutopian? Or to put the question another way, was digging at Yutopian the optimal way to learn more about the Early Formative period in the region? To be honest, at the time that question never occurred to me. I had, after all, been looking for a site at which to focus our excavations; excavation is a mode of inquiry I am trained in and comfortable with. On the other hand, I was quite concerned with whether Yutopian presented too many logistical issues. Jorge and his family had been extraordinarily gracious hosts (and medics) and made us feel welcome to work there, but Yutopian really *was* remote, with not even dirt roads for parts of the trip between Santa María and the site; logistics and communications would be difficult. Was this the site in which to invest so much time and effort?

In 1993, before I ended my visit to the Cajón, I was shown a second Formative site on the same west side of the valley, 8 km south of Yutopian. It was situated near the regional school, the church and the few houses that make up the community of La Quebrada, also important for being the terminus of the dirt road from Santa María. Two families in La Quebrada had pickup trucks which would radically facilitate travel and transport. And *this* site, Cardonal, was also large with much Early

Formative material on the surface and many undisturbed structures in evidence. Although lacking metal on the surface, this could have simply been sampling error. All of this made the original choice difficult. (We later did conduct excavations at Cardonal [see Bits 87–96] and it does appear to lack the diversity and richness of Yutopian's material culture, but this was just a hunch at the time.) In the end we excavated at Yutopian primarily because it held great promise for excellent new data on Formative society, but admittedly also because it seemed a lovely lucky place, we would be in excellent company with the Chaile family, it was a small enough community that we could employ everyone, and not entirely irrelevant: the views were excellent!

We now needed a provincial archaeology permit and, importantly, adequate funding to bring Argentinean–North American teams here to work. The project would have to be described in terms acceptable to local bureaucrats, regional managers of cultural patrimony and competitive US funding agencies and foundations. What could we say about wanting to dig here when we still knew so little about the site!? How could our gut excitement about Yutopian's archaeological potential, and the joy of finding ourselves in this spot, be coupled to current archaeological theory and methodology to sell ourselves and the site? What would make it an attractive project for foundations to support when they would never get to visit this place and savor its tremendous appeal?

Years later I still recall the brain strain of trying to recast the elegant site that held such Formative promise, the warm caring people and the long vistas, the sounds of roosters crowing, the broad fleshy cactus leaves and carefully tended peach trees, the homespun blankets and homemade pots, trying to translate all this into an abstract research question. To be honest, for us the site *was* an answer, not a question.

We decided to focus on the unusual variety of objects and different raw materials that we had seen on the surface, especially the classic Formative pottery types and the hammered bronze pieces. And we hoped the site would back us up if we argued that we might be seeing an actual Early Formative village here, and not the dispersed, low-density homesteads we kept reading about. Building on Cristina's bibliography and library survey of all the research previously done in the region, I wrote North American grant applications:

> In the chronology of Andean (Northwest) Argentina, Formative culture (400 BC–600 CE) is characterized as segmentary, egalitarian and self-sufficient, with strong regional or microregional characteristics (Olivera 1988:87; Ottonello y Lorandi 1987:67ff.; Tarragó n.d.). Low-density settlements typically consist of dispersed, undifferentiated individual or clus-

tered domestic structures, freestanding or with walled agricultural fields adjoining them (Berberián 1989; Raffino 1991:4; Scattolin 1990). Yet in the central area of Northwest Argentina the circulation of exotic goods, including complex ceramics like Condorhuasi polychromes and Candelaria modeled wares, copper and gold adornments, and bracelets and bells of bronze, is well documented for the Formative period (Scattolin 1990; Scattolin and Williams 1992). How these specialized goods functioned in the egalitarian context of Formative society, and what the context of production and consumption might have been for such goods, has not been questioned.

Our interest in the Formative, then, focuses on how specialized goods articulate with a model of Formative life that is characterized as replicative, egalitarian and gendered. At the household level in small-scale societies, with low densities of alienable goods, non-market distribution systems, and unspecialized, unconcentrated labor, how are we to understand the lateral cycling of specially crafted "surplus energy" products? Specifically, the links between the production of a small class of elaborated material culture and the everyday processing of agricultural products needs to be examined in terms of distinct (or overlapping) facilities, production regimes and social relations of production that would have guided each production arena. How these contrastive/compatible production routines, singly or together, would have maintained, reinforced or transformed gender relations in the context of Formative society is valuable to consider. . . .

The grant applications felt distant, even arbitrary and invented, compared to the deeply personal experiences at Yutopian. The proposals assured the granting commissions of scholarly purpose and well-prepared intellectual history; they fairly bristled with the authority of knowledge production in the hands of well-trained professionals. But the passionate memories of the site still resonated strongly. For the moment they sat side by side, intellectual curiosity and personal pleasure, both contributing to a growing keenness to explore further at Yutopian.

In several months' time, the Fulbright grant was awarded and Yutopian research was scheduled to begin.

10

SOCIO-POLITICS

Should North American archaeologists dig in Argentina?

Applying for research funds for Yutopian made me consider the large number of North American agencies and foundations that exist to fund North American archaeological projects abroad. In fact, there is a long distinguished history of Euro-American projects in the Andes— and even specifically in Northwest Argentina. Pioneering investigators from North America and Europe have contributed to understanding the prehistory of NOA (Bennett et al. 1948; Métraux 1930; Nordenskiöld 1903; Ten Kate 1893; Uhle 1912, 1923; Willey 1946, 1971), and such studies have continued into the present (Cornell 1993; D'Altroy et al. 2000; DeMarrais 1997; Johansson 1996; Pollard 1983). As well, Argentineans have trained in North America (González 1955, 1963; Nielsen 1996a, 1996b; Núñez Regueiro 1998). The list could be longer, but the point is clear: a handful of rich and powerful nations (mostly my own country—the United States—as well as Canada, several western European nations and Japan) undertake prehistoric research outside their national borders, developing the initial chronological sequences and establishing the logic of archaeology as the dominant scientific paradigm. At the same time, archaeologists of less-developed countries travel to the western centers to be trained in this logic and these methods but conduct their own research almost entirely within their own national borders.

The "archaeology-exporting" nations are also among the wealthiest industrial nation-states, controlling raw resource extraction from all corners of the world, mobilizing inexpensive labor to make the commodities we covet, consuming disproportionate amounts of energy, and disproportionately polluting the planet. Perhaps we should not be surprised to recognize that the international research programs we archaeologists design are often carried out in low-income countries, sometimes among the least-developed and lowest-income countries—countries that utilize the least amount of the world's energy and contribute the least pollution.

With all our sophistication at recognizing colonialist enterprises, the parallel is surely evident: archaeological resources (such as sites and archaeological labor) are exploited in less-developed countries just like other raw materials we use to make our lives convenient and pleasing. We who conduct international archaeology take what we can at the lowest cost and least effort to ourselves, following the same capitalist principles as in our nations' other extractive activities.

Of course international researchers are not simply callous capitalists out to maximize research gain and minimize project costs, and many instances of colleagues' highly ethical conduct and extraordinary generosity are known to us, in service to the administrative structures of host countries, to the communities in which guest researchers work, and to fellow scholars and students in host countries. Nevertheless, the asymmetrical global arrangements that underpin international research make great injustices possible, and the minimal standards of behavior set by host countries in their permitting requirements do not prevent these from happening: excavated materials are left in disarray; neither field reports nor field notes are filed with the excavated collections; no results are published in the language of the host country; local scholars are not kept informed or—worse yet—become angry about perceived infractions of agreements.

Sometimes I am asked, in the Santa María schools or even in the Valle del Cajón communities, why I have come from North America to do research here. I answer that this is one of few places in the world where the origins and "rise" of an autochthonous state (the Inka) can be studied. We can argue that the Andes have special significance in regard to cultural evolution and the human condition, that studying Andean prehistory is too important to be restricted to scientists from a single country. Just as UNESCO strives to protect significant cultural heritage in different nations of the world, so too should the Andes be open to investigation from different national perspectives.

But this argument doesn't convince people. They know rather that it is the powerful financial and scholarly resources of First World states (e.g., their libraries, advanced scientific equipment, research foundations, publication opportunities), backed by greater hegemonic power, that rationalize Euro-American scholars' domination of the research regions of the underdeveloped world. Commonly, at least part of the material results of such research comes to be housed in European and North American museums and universities, and the archaeological publications accumulate far from the people who today live near these sites.

Until recently this situation required no justification; practitioners like Heinrich Schliemann and Mortimer Wheeler provided models for conducting archaeological investigations in the heat and dust of underdeveloped countries, and generations of researchers from privileged countries followed in their footsteps. But today it is not so easy to rationalize continuing to work in other people's past and training students to do the same. The critique of continuing imperialistic forms of archaeological practice takes form around two related perceptions: (1) Archaeology is a manner of accruing power, of control over information that is extracted like any resource that destroys the context it comes from (oil, minerals, etc.). Its undertaking requires, perpetuates and intensifies unequal power as does any extractive enterprise performed by the core in the periphery; (2) archaeology provides a particular logic, one of any number, for charting the past, and the imposition of this logic— this specific impersonal manner of viewing the past through its material remains—is often not the accustomed manner of accounting for the past in other regions of the world. Thus the imperialist archaeologist not only takes pieces of the past away from the countries s/he visits, but at the same time forces an unfamiliar means of recounting (pre)history onto a still developing country (Gero 2006).

From this perspective, how do I come to terms with my own practices? Even while I admit to the deep pleasure of traveling to, living in and working in places that surprise and delight me every day, and relish the opportunity to explore their contemporary as well as their ancient social arrangements, is it ethical? How do I live with myself, conscious as I am of the inherent contradictions of doing archaeology in less advantaged countries than my own? What can I say?

Is it enough to argue that I try extremely hard to do it well? To point out that throughout the Yutopian project, I worked closely with an Argentinean collaborator, although we sometimes talked past one another and ultimately may not have been successful as a team? Does it help that we trained both Argentinean and North American students on our project, hoping they would establish long-term research partnerships? And that we tried to enrich the communities in which we worked, with museum exhibits and frequent public talks about what we did, with meaningful material gifts and good pay? Whom do we ask if we were acceptable in what we did, in how we worked and what we accomplished? Whose opinion counts?

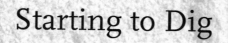

Starting to Dig

11

ARGUMENT

The positionality of practice

The data and ultimately the knowledge produced at Yutopian were thoroughly conditioned by the practices we employed, a fact made clear to us early in the project. That Cristina and I had been trained in different fieldwork traditions was not surprising, and we were prepared to find that we brought different techniques to the investigations. What was not clear at the outset, however, were the links between how we each practiced archaeology and how we each thereby contributed to a different sort of knowledge.

As is common in Argentina, Cristina had been involved more in survey work than excavations, and the excavation focus I brought to Yutopian was somewhat uncomfortable to Cristina who regretted not having broader knowledge about the Formative landscape of the Valle del Cajón. On the other hand my feminist perspectives were better served by excavations that could reveal the intimacies of everyday life. In the end the matter was resolved for us by a simple administrative coup in which the provincial administrator of cultural heritage allowed us excavation rights only at Yutopian and Cardonal, but no further permission to survey (Bit 75).

As soon as we began mapping at Yutopian, we discovered that our foundational practices were hugely different. Without giving it much thought, I employed my familiar tripod-ed instruments to read in a N-S baseline, the longest on which a grid could be constructed, and staked it off at 20-m intervals. At the same time Cristina began an organic map of the structures, working from point to point with a hand-held compass and tapes, constantly checking herself with back readings. Cristina worked from what she encountered on the ground whereas my map was imposed on the topography of the site, starting with the longest continuous north-south line that could be shot down the length of the Yutopian ridge with the transit, and adjusted 30° west from a true N-S bearing to create a "map north-south" line. We then shot in "map east-west" lines at right angles to our baseline to reach the edges of the ridgetop, thus completing a grid on which we could plot Cartesian reference points for anywhere on site. Our perspective was situated in a contemporary instrumented landscape, a framework of our own creation having nothing to do with how the landscape had been occupied in Formative times. We had erected a standardized organizational framework and would put the "knowledge" into it.

Meanwhile, Cristina's "sketch map" was made more quickly, while we were still shooting in baselines. This map directly reproduced the structures and their relations to one another, and her representation was so accurate that we could locate any point on the ridgetop by measuring compass angles and distances to the nearest structure. There were no arbitrary reference points or lines that originated with the researcher rather than from the site itself; the site was not abstracted as a surface to be investigated but rather reflected the visible patterns of Formative life on the ground. All the reference points for this knowledge are internal to the knowledge itself. When we later brought in a total mapping station with its laser and digital accuracy to record the topography, structures and placement of our archaeological work, we found it somewhat less accurate than Cristina's map because the sophisticated mappers were not familiar with the site or with Formative archaeology in the region and simply couldn't determine the best mapping points to fix with their state-of-the-art equipment (Fig. 24).

We also encountered "positional" differences in analysis, again fixed by our distinct conventions of practice and underpinned by different foundational logics. I assumed charge of the analysis of lithic materials, while Cristina organized the ceramic analysis. I immediately came up with a standardized form on which to record information from every excavated stratum. Each bag of lithic material was to be sorted into discrete raw material categories and then into size categories (which had to be juggled until we found categories that produced the most balanced counts). Tools were separated out in a different column, and distinctive tools were traced on the back of the analysis sheets. Meanwhile, Cristina and her students located all the ceramic sherds that retained a portion of the vessel rim and drew each ceramic profile individually, recording and preserving its integrity. The only categorical notation that Cristina made was to assign each sherd to either "coarse ware," "intermediate ware" or "fine ware" depending on the paste, temper and surface finish.[1]

Part of the difference in analytical practice here emerges out of the different materials we assigned ourselves to analyze. Stone is less likely to suffer post-depositional transformation or fracture, and thus its size and raw material correspond more closely to how it appeared and was used in prehistory. In contrast, ceramic sherds bear little resemblance to the sizes and shapes in which they were first produced and used, so recording simple standardized attributes is more difficult. Still, if I had been analyzing the ceramics, I'm sure I would have constructed

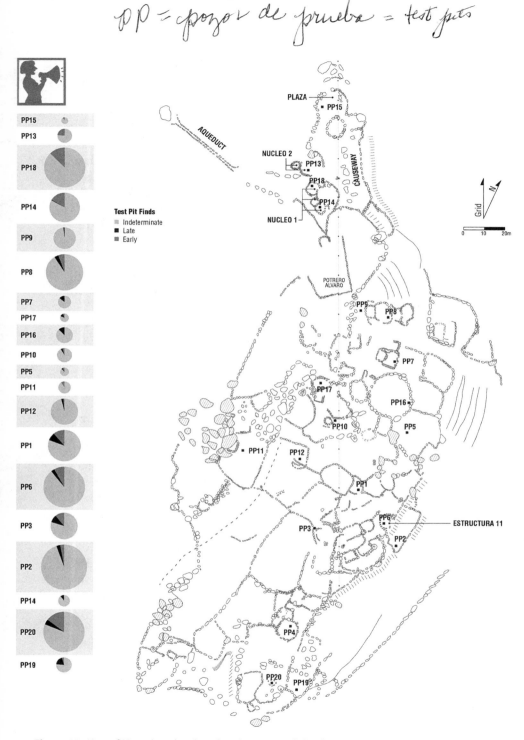

Figure 24. Map of Yutopian showing the placement of the first 20 test pits, with test pit results. Note also the location of excavation areas during subsequent field seasons.

abstracted categories to "describe" the paste, temper and surface finish, perhaps thickness of sherd, decoration, et cetera. The contrast in analytical styles is similar to what we had observed in mapping. While I extracted knowledge in my own heavily constructed categories, Cristina hewed closely to the actual Formative forms, imposing little of her world on them.

There were surely other instances at Yutopian where contrasting archaeological practices revealed different underlying logics, but I noted only one more. When I encountered what I called an archaeological "feature," I found to my surprise that Argentinean archaeologists have no generalized word for a nonspecific archaeological anomaly, perhaps again because the notion of a "feature" is abstracted from the specifics of the archaeological record, and in Argentina the archaeological "record" is not an abstract idea; here are only the physical remains themselves.

It is tempting to ponder the cultural—or political—utility of these practices, their practical origins in different contexts. How much was my scientific training tied to a conveniently homogenizing view of the world configured by issues of control and extraction? More speculatively, how much does Cristina's training—and the worldview that gives rise to it—serve to protect and give meaning to the specifics and the uniqueness of her historic national context?

These are speculations perhaps, but I argue that here and elsewhere in our international collaborative project we found ourselves working within the constraints of different research logics; that the scientific paradigm in which I worked did not derive from more expensive or precise equipment, nor from a determination to be accurate. Cristina was more accurate and precise than I was. But I worked relative to sampling spaces, hypotheses, views of social change and abstracted populations that were external to the past we recovered, while Cristina worked within a prehistory that originated in, and was conditioned by, the traces of the past that we recovered. I am sure our understandings of the past were both enriched and frustrated by this complementarity.

Note

1. Cristina regularly assigned sherds to typological classes, but during our wrap-up season of laboratory analysis, her organizing summation for recording ceramics consisted of drawing vessel profiles.

 **12**

EPISODE

Digging test pits

By the time we arrived back at Yutopian in 1994, I had a Fulbright award to teach archaeology at the University of Catamarca and alternately to work at Yutopian, and Cristina had assembled a team of Argentinean archaeology students interested in "Northwest research": Juan Leoni, Laura Pérez Jimeno and Hugo Puentes. We converged in Santa María in March, a wonderful autumnal season in the mountains, windy and clear and considerably warmer than my 1993 July–August survey. I was the only *yanqui*.

Cristina began by mapping Yutopian, although at times we didn't understand how specific wall segments were related. Simultaneously we started to lay out and excavate our first *pozos de prueba* (test pits) in order to understand the fundamental composition of the site: the depth and density of cultural deposits across the site, and the relative frequency and distribution of Early Formative remains (Fig. 25). Interestingly, my field journal from 1993, my first visit to Yutopian, already notes some distributional hunches:

> [July 21] Moving to the southern end of the site, there is better preservation across the entire ridge width, even showing some enclosures and walls on the west side, in contrast to the steep east slopes of the ridgetop. Also it *appears* (emphasis in original) that the frequency of red sherds and black-on-red painted sherds increases moving south, almost as though the earliest Formative parts [of the site] were "near" the height of the hilltop, where I observed esp nice circular recintos and no immediately apparent "red" sherds at all!

Although I had thought I observed an early-late distributional pattern in 1993, it was necessary in 1994 to document my casual observations and see how rigidly they obtained. Placing 1 × 1 m test pits across the site was my North American strategy, but this technique is not regularly used in Argentinean archaeology where researchers are more likely to place single *sondage* units after careful surface inspections. Certainly

Figure 25. Opening the first *pozos de prueba* (test pits) (PPs 4 and 13).

how we tested the site fundamentally conditioned what we later came to know about Yutopian and, ultimately, about the Early Formative.

We had little interest in applying a random sampling program to our test pits at Yutopian; rather, we wanted the *pozos de prueba* (test pits) to yield stratigraphic and distributional information across the site as well as to provide first clues in other lines of inquiry: could we identify functions of structures, discriminating between residences, patios, storage areas and walled gardens? What would we be able to learn about domestic economies? Were domestic structures swept clean or did they accumulate material? Could we locate middens? And ultimately, was gendered labor revealed in households?

We dug twenty 1 × 1 m *pozos* in March, distributed as shown in Figure 24 and in Table 1. My explicit interest in households and the arrangements of household economies guided the placement of *pozos* inside and around structures. We placed the first five pits where architectural remains were most dense, between 50 and 150 m south of our datum, but we encountered mostly mixed materials and altogether fewer Formative diagnostic ceramics. The next five pits only extended the tested area to 12 m north of our datum. By Pozo de Prueba 13 (PP 13), however, we understood that we needed to test much farther north along the baseline because Formative materials systematically came from the northern part of the site. Ultimately we covered the entire 300-m length of the baseline.

We dug all *pozos* in arbitrary levels of 10 cm because we didn't yet know what the stratigraphy would look like. We quickly learned, however, that the well-drained soils of the ridgetop and terraces had suffered severe leaching over the millennia, and no traces of occupational lenses or other organic soil color changes were visible, apart from fire discolorations. All excavated materials were screened in ⅛-inch screens except when we needed to put extra screens into service and were forced to employ our only ¼-inch screen as well. Test pit depths varied from 30 to 110 cm depending on whether we found ourselves inside a semi-subterranean structure or outside where bedrock was encountered after removing only a 20- to 30-cm level of topsoil.

Testing was exciting; it was our first look at the prehistoric material in context, an intense learning period for us all: co-directors, crew, students and Chailes alike. Where test pits did not quickly peter out, the loamy soils in the upper three or four levels still frequently failed to produce noteworthy or diagnostic materials until suddenly in the fourth or fifth level, around 50 cm below ground surface, we would encounter higher percentages of finely made decorated pottery, larger pieces of animal bone and diverse lithic materials, including obsidian and colored cherts. Polished slate knives always came from lower levels as well. Sometimes the levels with quantities of interesting materials would occur just above bedrock, but sometimes these artifact-bearing levels extended another 40 or even 50 cm before bedrock. This was all valuable input for planning the larger excavation blocks. On the other hand, each test pit risked destroying the integrity of a larger archaeological unit, taking a bite out of the floor of a structure just to get a taste.

Some test pits were placed deliberately to check for early or late occupations while others were placed to understand specific features of the site. The floor of PP 12, in what we thought was an area of cultivation, revealed a sharply defined diagonal line dividing bedrock on one side and a charcoal-laden pit on the other, with large quantities of burnt material and charcoal (Bit 53 and Fig. 75). One of the walls of PP 13 cut a vertical profile straight through a pit that had been dug into the bedrock, with a grinding stone and another large flat rock in it.

The challenge in the test pit phase was to keep selecting locations for and staking out future test pits before they were needed so that no one was standing around waiting for something to do. While PP 12, 13 and 14 were being worked on, Cristina and I laid out PP 16, 17 and 18, later adding 19 and 20 to get to the southernmost extreme, and then we decided to stop and see where we were.

13

RAW DATA

What the test pits told us

Table 1. Ceramic counts from 1994 test pits, arranged north to south

Test Pit #	Grid Location (north–south)	Test Pit Placement on Site	Total Depth (from surface to bedrock)	Total Ceramics Recovered	Early Diagnostic Ceramics	Late Diagnostic Ceramics
15	117N × 9W	north plaza	18 cm	10	1	—
13	85N × 16W	in small round enclosure (Estructura 5)	70 cm	38	9	—
18	77N × 13W	in small round enclosure (Estructura 1)	110 cm	356	44	—
14	66N × 10W	in small round enclosure (Estructura 3)	68 cm	196	32	1
9	12N × 10E	outside a group of enclosures	30 cm	104	—	2
8	10N × 24E	in large round enclosure	60 cm	289	16	10
7	10S × 27E	in double-walled rectangular enclosure	45 cm	35	—	5
17	25S × 9W	in double-walled rectangular enclosure	30 cm	16	1	2
16	31S × 32E	in large central round enclosure	64 cm	58	—	7
10	44S × 3W	central area between enclosures	30 cm	43	—	1
5	50S × 33E	in double-walled small enclosure	30 cm	16	1	1
11	60S × 48W	between enclosures	40 cm	29	3	
12	64S × 20W	adjacent to poorly defined wall	60 cm	157	2	4
1	80S × 9E	in central oddly shaped enclosure	110 cm	227	25	18
6	97S × 22E	in small round enclosure	100 cm	364	29	10

Table 1. *Continued*

Test Pit #	Grid Location (north–south)	Test Pit Placement on Site	Total Depth (from surface to bedrock)	Total Ceramics Recovered	Early Diagnostic Ceramics	Late Diagnostic Ceramics
3	100S × 12W	in passageway between structures	40 cm	154	17	14
2	109S × 28E	on first terrace, east side of ridge	60 cm	448	12	12
4	150S × 25W	in large oval enclosure	40 cm	29	—	3
20	179S × 34W	on first terrace, south end	30 cm	361	53	15
19	183S × 22W	badly preserved architectural area	52 cm	51	2	10

Cristina organized a rough classification of the test pit ceramics right there in the field to see the distribution of early and late occupations across the Yutopian ridgetop. Moving rapidly through the excavated materials, she noted the distribution of familiar diagnostic sherds from each pit and level. If intact Formative occupations existed, where could they best be studied? A few cautionary points are needed here in interpreting her results.

- *Differential preservation of diagnostic ceramic features*: Most diagnostic Formative ceramics are thin-walled with polished surfaces readily recognized by sight and touch and not prone to erosion. Diagnostic ceramics of the Regional Development period (RDP) are generally thicker-walled and their unpolished exterior painted surfaces erode easily. If the diagnostic paint or postfire slips are missing, RDP ceramics in the field resemble general cookwares and are easily classified "indeterminate" and thus under-represented in final counts.
- *State of knowledge*: In this early stage of research we were not yet familiar with Yutopian ceramics, and certainly when I participated in ceramic counts I didn't understand that both the Tosco Pulido (polished coarseware) and the Tosco Engobe Rojo (red-slipped coarseware) are (or can be) Formative. We were also unfamiliar with the Yutopian Formative style of Baño Blanco (white postfire slips). In hindsight, our early ignorance under-represented Formative ceramics.
- *Research focus*: In large ceramic counts, especially early on, we concentrated specifically on noting whether Formative materials were

included in each level (present or absent). The upper levels of PP 2, for instance, show no "late" materials, almost certainly because we were more interested in looking specifically for Formative sherds.

Despite these biases, several patterns clearly emerge:

- Test pits at the northern end of the site produced only early (Formative) ceramics.
- Formative ceramics appeared everywhere on the ridgetop, in the north and the south.
- The late period (RDP) ceramics came almost exclusively—and in much higher numbers—from the southern test pits.
- Test pits in the center of the ridge invariably showed RDP ceramics overlying Formative ceramics.

To test this pattern, Hugo and Álvaro excavated two additional test pits, PP 19 and 20, at the extreme southern end of the site (183S 22W and 179S 34W), and it held for the most part: we recovered tiny black-on-red painted sherds and a tiny triangular (late) obsidian projectile point in these southernmost pits. But while I would have preferred otherwise (my lust for unambiguous patterns being deeply conditioned), I must force myself to admit there was also some Formative material in PP 20.

14

NARRATIVE

The incredible Pozo de Prueba 18

Juan had dug 80 cm into PP 18 before he spied the glint of trowel on stone and saw the upper curved edge of a substantial horizontally placed grinding stone. Known locally as a *conana*, it is often associated with grinding corn, although other foods can be pulverized in it to make sauces or flours (Bit 94). By 90 cm it was completely uncovered and we were dazzled by the big (17 cm) polished mano set within the concavity of the *conana*, seemingly undisturbed over the perhaps 1700 years since the coupled implements were last used (Fig. 26).

Figure 26. Pozo de Prueba 18 framing a large horizontal grinding stone (*conana*) and mano in situ on the occupation floor. PP 18 was later incorporated into Estructura 1, Unit 301.

When we placed this test pit within an arbitrarily selected, well-formed northern *recinto*, of course we couldn't know what lay beneath the surface, so it was truly amazing that our 1 × 1 m *pozo* managed to come down upon and contain the entire grinding stone. Equally impressive was that the mano looked as if it had just been laid there for a moment while the grinder stepped away to take care of other business. Such placement is neither casual nor disturbed, so with great excitement we could now conclude that Yutopian contained at least some intact structures with utensils left in place on occupation floors.

In my public accounts of work at Yutopian I make much of this find. I generally say that our excavation plan fell into place after our incredible luck finding a *conana* complete with its associated mano in their "original" functional positions in PP 18. The logic is clear and compelling and the outcome of how we came to excavate our first structure is neatly explained: we proceeded to excavate Estructura 1 based on what we learned from PP 18. And so it was, but slightly more complicated.

15

EPISODE

Extending test pit excavations

Here's the truth. After we had located the compelling and intact *conana* in PP 18, we did not actually begin to excavate the occupation floor on which it lay. The linear story is a convenient abbreviation, skipping over a difficult, ambiguous time to create a more elegant economical account of our practices.

What actually unfolded was messier because we still weren't *ready* to establish a large excavation block, even after the *conana* was exposed. In fact, PP 18 showed only a few artifacts in association with the *conana*, none of them distinctly Formative, plus we were still unsure at that point about the spatial distribution of Formative versus RDP occupations along the ridge. Finally, we needed to account for the fact that from what we had seen so far, we hadn't located any clear RDP occupation and virtually all of our excavated diagnostic material was Formative, despite the fact that our extensive surface collecting had included many later period ceramics. We definitely needed to speed up artifact washing to classify the test pit ceramics, so we opted to move in two directions: while Cristina organized a washing and classifying team, I would open up contiguous excavation units in two different areas of the site where Formative materials had seemed abundant.

We had placed PP 6 inside a semi-round or sub-rectangular structure that sat amid other well-defined structures midway along the ridge (97 m south) on its eastern slope (22 m east of the baseline), with terraces falling off sharply below the structure on the east. The 1 × 1 m test pit had yielded a broken *conana* and polished mano in the level 40–50 cm below surface (bs) associated with little diagnostic material. But below that, in Level 8, between 70–80 cm bs, many Formative diagnostic sherds had been recovered, together with llama bones and an obsidian biface stem. This seemed to promise enough Formative material to identify a Formative occupation, possibly an occupation floor, so I decided to open three additional 1 × 1 m test units around PP 6 to form a 2 × 2 m excavation block. We tentatively called this area Sector I.

Meanwhile, the crew who had worked on PP 3 had also recovered impressive quantities of Formative material. This test pit (100S 12W) had been placed between two walls that appeared to define a passageway littered with surface material including polished greyware pottery and obsidian flakes. Although the test pit had only gone down 30 cm and had both early and late period ceramics, there was sufficient Formative material to test further. We had also found fragments of what seemed to be a human cranium in the shallow fill. We first laid out two adjacent 1 × 1 m units and then expanded this area yet another 3 m², so that in the end the five additional 1 × 1 m excavation units contiguous to PP 3 were referred to as Sector II.

While Cristina concentrated on analyzing the frequencies and distributions of test pit ceramics (among other things), crews spent five days working in Sectors I and II, using notes from the first test pit in each sector as a guide to where to expect Formative materials. Our goal in these expanded test pit sectors was to locate clearly defined Formative occupations interesting and extensive enough to warrant a large block excavation and meanwhile allow us bigger pictures of the spatial arrangements of artifacts within the tested zones to perhaps offer clues to the functional use of space.

We learned a lot from Sector I: that the house we were excavating had a clear double occupation with large coarse and combed ceramics down to 50 cm bs, a level rather empty of finds between 60 and 80 cm bs, and a clear Formative occupation below 80 cm where the finds continued below the (apparently later, remodeled) external wall but where there was only one late sherd. We also learned that the bedrock levels and the living floors sloped down toward the centers of the structures and that the external walls sometimes sloped outward, causing Álvaro to comment, "We are in a *tasa* [cup]!" (We were to learn later that this last feature, walls that sloped outward at the top, was most surely a feature of remodeling houses in later periods.) Altogether this was a satisfying expansion of a test unit, giving us the sense of gaining knowledge.

Sector II on the other hand, with considerable investment of time and effort, was less satisfying. The expanded area now included both the PP 3 "passageway" space and part of the interior of the adjacent structure. My March 12 notes remind me: "Clearly diagnostic Formative pieces from the upper levels of excavations and NO late pieces from the excavations, despite a heavy scatter of late pieces on the surface!" But as we removed the stones of the inner "passageway" wall (that is, the actual wall of the structure), we unexpectedly began to uncover the remains of a shallow burial, scapula first, then ribs, then arms doubled under the body (see Bit 16). The lack of a prepared burial chamber or special preparation of the body left few clues and had given no warning of this development. Clearly the burial had been placed before the wall was built.

Many questions arose: Who was this person? Could s/he be associated with the building of the wall? Or were the wall and the burial later and intrusive into an otherwise early context? Or had the burial, passageway and structure all been occupied first during the Early Formative occupation and then reoccupied in a later Formative time, or even in the RDP? Could we isolate where the Early Formative material was coming from? Whew, what a surprise!

As we reached 40–50 cm bs, large surface-combed and black/red/white painted Santamariana sherds appeared associated with the burial, along with a slightly deeper Aguada (Late Formative) sherd, clearly a mixed fill rather than a true depositional stratigraphy. But below these, where soil only remained in pockets of the bedrock, we found a few polished and incised grey and buff Early Formative sherds. The burial now seemed a later intrusion into an originally Early Formative context, with much mixing of levels, but there was one more surprise for us here: a well-formed elongated pit dug obliquely into the bedrock beneath an overhanging bedrock lip, and from this pit, positioned roughly directly under where the burial had been, we extracted several large stone tools, a stemmed obsidian projectile point, a round mano, several large ceramic sherds, some bone and a slate knife, all diagnostically early. At first we tried to relate the pit to the burial, thinking that the intrusive burial had taken advantage of a convenient chamber-like pit in the earlier house floor to deposit the dead . . . but the rock overhang "ceiling" made this improbable, and the relation between the lower pit and the intrusive burial was evidently more complicated.

Some resolution came as we opened more of the area inside the structural walls: shallow deposits here proved consistently mixed with only a slight tendency for early materials to occur lower down. We were also learning from the house excavations that we were calling Sector I; in contrast to this mixed fill, the Sector I house excavations showed more clearly stratigraphic deposits, enabling us to extrapolate patterns: at least some Sector II houses were reoccupied, their floors sloped toward the centers of the structures, dish-like, and deposits were quite shallow near the walls where we had started. But the relationship of the Sector II passageway and its heavy Early Formative fill to the rest of the excavation area was not resolved. It was both messy and frustrating as workmen and students had to learn to trowel patiently, to look for subtle soil variations, and to recognize pottery types and architectural variations that none of us had ever seen before.

With more field seasons behind me now, I am convinced that the "passageway" was a Formative-style entranceway where, instead of offering a simple opening in a wall, the wall on one side of the doorway is made to overlap in front of the other side of the doorway to create a "double wall" following the curved contour of the structure. Had we dug further here, we would understand more about which parts of the early architecture were modified and which left untouched, and maybe even understand why walls more than a meter thick would be erected here at a relatively small settlement. But recognizing the discomforting messiness of mixed occupations, we abandoned this area and never resolved its cultural and architectural sequences.

16

ANDEAN WAYS

Inadvertent human remains

During our first (1994) field season at Yutopian Jorge Chaile and I were working together in Unit 201 when we realized we were uncovering an unexpected human burial, and frankly I was horrified. This was the last thing I wanted to find, and I was especially uncomfortable with Jorge right beside me. I hated the idea of digging up other people's ancestors, and my interests were truly in households, not burials. I shuddered and put down my trowel. "Whoa, Jorge. Let's stop right here."

I laid out our options: We could simply cover up what we'd uncovered and relocate our excavations to another area. OR if Jorge preferred we could carefully remove the bones however he recommended and rebury them at another location—on site or elsewhere—with an appropriate ceremony. OR, and this seemed unwise to me, we could continue to excavate and treat the bones like any other archaeological evidence. I wanted Jorge to make this decision, and I tried to make it clear that I was not at all invested in this test excavation, that it was merely part of having a good look at different parts of the site.

Jorge surprised me. He insisted we collect the bones, put them in a box and continue digging, no problem. "Are you sure, Jorge??? It really doesn't matter to me!" I repeated several times in my most sincere Spanish. No, he insisted, it was fine to dig up the bones because, he explained, this was not a Christian, this was (merely) a pagan! Clearly the product of a missionary education, Jorge played it cool, surely saying what he thought I wanted to hear and not yet a good enough friend to negotiate a new plan.

But the next morning as we started work, Jorge asked me if I'd heard whistling during the night. Both he and Ramona had heard it for long stretches all night, passing down the valley from north to south, passing close to Yutopian and lingering near our encampment. This had nothing to do with "pagans"; in many Andean accounts whistling is associated with the dead who are moving near us (e.g., Allen 1988:60; Walter 2006:178). Obviously Jorge was altogether less sure than he'd first let on that the skeletal remains were neutralized by their pre-Christian associations. It was the only time in the many years I subsequently worked with Jorge that he talked of having heard whistling.

At the end of this stint of fieldwork, the boxed bones were moved to the archaeology lab in Catamarca. Later, as we learned more about the site, we recognized they represented a later intrusive burial, and I'm afraid we've never had them identified or studied further.

17

EPISODE

Opening Estructura Uno

Given the results of the ceramic classification from the test pits, we were encouraged to return to PP 18 with its perfectly framed *conana* grinding stone, counting on the fact that since it lay at the northern end of the site, it would be Early Formative (Fig. 27). (In fact, from here on we mostly worked in the northern part of the site.) We extended PP 18 aggressively by digging three side-by-side 2 × 2 m test units to surround it and we took our time; Jorge, Álvaro and Federico—plus Ramona who had been washing ceramics—had all gone off to round up cows for vaccination (see Bit 20). Our idea was to expose the entire northern third of this partially buried structure, combining the new 2 × 2 m units with PP 18.

Based on PP 18, we could expect the occupation floor—or *an* occupation floor—to correspond to the depth at which the *conana* lay, around 95 cm bs. But more recent floors could also be discovered above this

Estructura 4

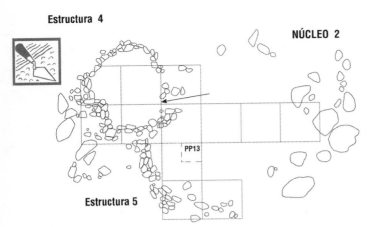

NÚCLEO 2

PP13

Estructura 5

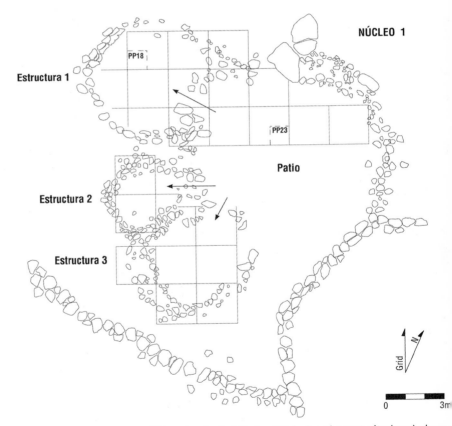

NÚCLEO 1

Estructura 1

PP18

PP23

Patio

Estructura 2

Estructura 3

Grid
N

0   3m

Figure 27. Map of the northern sector of Yutopian (called Sector III during the test pit phase) show-ing Núcleo 1 (Estructuras 1, 2 and 3) and Núcleo 2 (Estructuras 4 and 5).

Figure 28. Opening Units 300, 301 and 302 in Estructura 1.

one, floors that would have been easy to miss in the 1 × 1 m *pozo* and which would show up more readily in the larger exposed block. Digging in pairs, a student with a *lugareño* (local workman) in each 2 × 2 m unit, the crew began by removing the upper 25 cm of fill by shovel shaving and thereafter troweling in 10-cm arbitrary levels (Fig. 28). From the beginning, we found no late (RDP) ceramics or any indicators that were not consistent with an Early Formative occupation, even within the upper strata of fill.

As we gradually uncovered the stone wall defining the north side of the structure, it struck me that different construction patterns were evident in different places along this wall. At first I worried that the wall at lower levels was not continuous, that this wasn't an enclosure at all but just disassociated wall segments, since both the curvature of the wall and the pattern of stone constructions varied from unit to unit. As we went deeper, the continuity of the wall was apparent, but we have never understood why the north and northeastern arcs of the wall were built in a formal pattern of alternating large and small stones (Fig. 29), while the same curvature and stoneworking pattern are not continued throughout the enclosing structural wall.

The depositional variation we encountered proved to be typical of the entire structure: The first 50–60 cm contained little cultural material, and what did appear was fragmented and eroded. From 60 to 90 cm,

Figure 29. Construction pattern of northern wall of Estructura 1. Note the bottom of PP 18 still visible in the floor.

the cultural material increased but lacked structural associations and contained no complete tools or artifacts. Between 90 and 110 cm, however, we encountered a wealth of evidence for an occupation floor.

As used here, "occupation floor" combines the idea of a "living floor"—a level surface on which humans carried out activities at a given time—with the notion of an "occupation," referring to a period of time in which a given people occupied an area or a house. Since the floor in Estructura 1 varies in depth between 90 and 110 cm, and not all of this variation is accounted for by the floor sloping inward toward the center (saucer-style), it remains true that we recovered artifacts from slightly different depths within a shallow "floor" of activity.

Multiple lines of evidence for the occupation floor showed up in these initial three units of Estructura 1 (Fig. 30):

- In addition to the horizontal *conana* identified in PP 18, we encountered three more grinding stones in the same quadrant of the house, two inclined on their sides and the third one laid flat as the first had been. Although these were all clustered in the northeast quadrant of the floor, their depths varied in relation to their distance from the center of the structure, the lowest ones being closest to the center;

- Whereas upper levels contained only sherds, flakes and bone fragments, the occupation floor yielded many whole tools and artifacts;
- A whole unbroken bowl had been inverted and inclined against the wall (Bit 19);
- We identified smoothed or flat consolidations of burnt clay adhering to the base of the north and northwestern portions of the wall, apparently the remains of a plastered floor; and
- The occupation floor at 90–110 cm (including the whole ceramic vessels and whole bone artifacts) does not appear to have been as disturbed as it would have been had subsequent living floors been occupied above it.

Not only was there an occupation floor, but it included a rich material inventory at this level and it was minimally disturbed (that is, it had excellent integrity of deposition), promising great interpretive opportunities. We left the depth of these excavation units at the level of the occupation floor (rather than going all the way down to bedrock) and designated this structure Estructura 1 and the cluster of structures within which it was standing as Núcleo 1 (or Patio Group 1).

Figure 30. Grinding stone and fractured black bowl (Figure 32) positioned on the occupation floor of Estructura 1, Units 300 and 301 at 110 cm. Note pieces of the plaster floor adhering to structure walls.

Knowledge-Production Facts

- The first three units of Estructura I were gridded out, excavated and photographed in five working days by three *lugareños*, two co-directors and three Argentinean students.
- Seventy-eight bags of ceramic, lithic and bone material were collected from an area that measured approximately 9 m² (without PP 18).
- Sixty-five sheets of paper, including field journals, excavation unit forms, feature forms and catalog information resulted from this work.
- Twenty-seven black-and-white photographs and 24 slides were taken during this work episode.

18

RAW DATA

Inventory of artifact counts and special finds from Units 300, 301 and 302

The volume of recovered artifacts from the first three excavated units (2 × 2 m) of what came to be known as Estructura I is given in Table 2a. Because our square units were imposed on a round structure, the units were actually different sizes (Unit 301 being the largest); because the floor of the structure was saucer-shaped, the depth of 301, the center unit, was also deeper than the others. Note that each excavated level is 10 cm deep.

Table 2a. Inventory of general artifact counts from Estructura 1, Units 300, 301 and 302

	UNIT 300			UNIT 301			UNIT 302			
	Ceramics	Stone	Bone	Ceramics	Stone	Bone	Ceramics	Stone	Bone	Depth bd
Level 1	103	35	9	171	61	42	158	74	26	0–50
Level 2	36	29	19	57	23	22	81	25	15	50–60
Level 3	46	24	29	100	55	83	92	51	20	60–70
Level 4	68	35	26	111	61	91	92	36	73	70–80
Level 5	67	46	59	103	49	75	64	39	99	80–90
Level 6	78	44	70	140	72	126	116	100	236	90–100
Level 7	60	39	63	114	80	143	106	75	129	100–110
Level 8	46	17	23	83	49	98	105	57	176	110–120
Level 9				76	46	121	104	52	122	120–130
Pits				20	32	60	31	24	60	
Total	504	329	320	975	528	861	949	533	956	

Note: Overall artifact densities are highest in the central unit (301) and at the levels just above the occupation floor, in Levels 6 and 7. The floor lies in Levels 7 and 8. Note the pit contents in Units 301 and 302.

Table 2b. Inventory of special finds from Estructura 1, Units 300, 301 and 302 (with special find numbers 1–10 relating to finds from the first 20 test pits, and special find numbers 11–20 relating to finds from Sectors I and II)

Special Find No.	Provenience	Depth	Material	Description	Figure No. (if illustrated)
21	301	1	ceramic	drilled pendant	
11	301	3	obsidian	projectile point	
12	302	4	bone	tubular bead (?)	
13	302	4	ceramic	Condorhuasi sherd	
14	300	5	??metal	bubbly material (scoria)	
15	302	5	??metal	bubbly material (scoria)	
18	300	7	ceramic	polished black bowl	Fig. 32
27	300	7	ceramic	disk	
16	301	7	ceramic	burnt clay mass	
28	300	8	ceramic	disk	
9	PP 18 (301)	8	ceramic	Condorhuasi sherd (mends with no. 57)	
25	301	8	ceramic	Condorhuasi sherd	
17	302	8	slate	flat, circular adornment	
19	302	8	ceramic	grey incised sherd (anthropomorhic)	
20	302	8	stone	cylindrical mortar	Fig. 49
22	301	9	basalt	projectile point	
23	302	9	bone	metapodial "spatula"	Fig. 31
26	301	9	stone	malachite chunk	
24	301	10	shell	eggshell frag. (suri)	

Note: Units 300, 301 and 302 each measured roughly 2 × 2 m, excavated to bedrock. The greatest density of finds is from Level 7 and below, pertaining to the occupation floor.

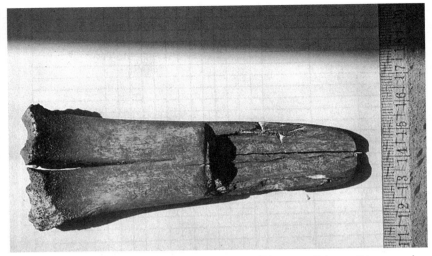

Figure 31. Bone tool ("spatula") made from a camelid metapodial, possibly a weaving implement, from Estructura 1, Unit 302 (Special Find 23).

Early in the project we adopted the practice of separating unique or rare objects from the generally bagged ceramic, bone and stone artifacts to help later in photographing and preparing objects for further analysis; each special find received a unique number in the excavation catalog. We tried to be consistent in what we designated a "special find" but didn't always succeed. Condorhuasi sherds, ground stone tools and projectile points were especially vulnerable to sometimes—and sometimes not—being treated as "special." An unsurpassed number of special finds were identified from the first three excavated units, including a large bone tool (Fig. 31).

NARRATIVE

Emotional moments

Working on the first excavations units of Estructura 1 was a continuous adrenalin rush. There was so much that was new to all of us as we came together for the first time on the project, working as a team in a single location toward a common goal. We were still learning each other's names for things, exchanging conventions for handling new situations, establishing organizational procedures on the spot. There were new soils, new pottery types, unfamiliar stratigraphy, different degrees and kinds of training, especially when we included the three *lugareños* who knew the soils better than any of us. It was intense . . . and fun.

As we worked down through the strata we became more proficient as a team . . . and the finds came at us faster and faster. At 85 cm bs we noticed something completely new again. "What is it, Jorge? ¿Que tienes allá? Dime ¿está de piedra o cerámica? ¿Pero que *pienses* puede ser? Well, what does it *seem* like to you???"

We always kept an eye on where Jorge was excavating because he often found exciting material, digging quickly but carefully. Now we were all huddled around his excavation unit in the northwest corner of Estructura 1 because he had announced he'd found something near the wall. Jorge seldom drew attention to himself unless he judged he had a very interesting thing to see; only a few minutes ago we had watched him uncover a second grinding stone in Estructura 1, less than a meter from the edge of PP 18 where the first grinding stone had been recovered, and now there was something else. Whatever it was, it was pushed right up against the structure wall, and it looked black or dark grey. I handed him a brush to work with, to replace his trowel, and he tried brushing the dirt away but it was packed solidly around the object and wouldn't easily brush away. He went back to his trowel and worked carefully; the faster he cleared the dirt away, the more we crowded around. It's ceramic, he told us, and broken; you can see the crack running across the surface here. But it looked very fine, very smooth, very highly polished . . . and quite large. As we watched, we cracked dumb jokes because we were nervous, excited: "Maybe it's Álvaro's lunch pail." "It's no fair, Jorge finds

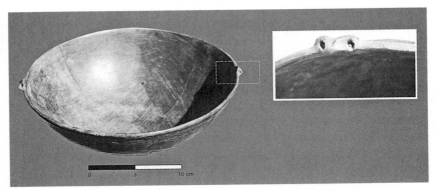

Figure 32. Polished black bowl from Estructura 1, Unit 300, with pinched rim suggesting animal heads on opposing sides (special find 18, see Table 2b).

all the good stuff. . . ." "I think Jorge plants stuff in his unit so he can find it in front of everyone!"

Then Jorge announced that it was a pot, turned upside down and leaned against the wall, complete but cracked in two (Fig. 32). Slowly he worked the dirt away from the sides, brushing and troweling, and finally he picked up the two large pieces, fitting them together with the rim upwards as it would be used. He handed it to me.

I was overwhelmed to receive it. Everyone was peering around and over my shoulders, and I held this beautiful bowl carefully so that the two pieces fit back together. It was very delicate, maybe 28 cm (11") across at the rim, with gently in-curving side walls and two little pinched animal faces on opposite sides of the rim. I was laughing and at the same time deeply moved, my heart pulled with the sheer emotion of having this 1700-year-old bowl in my hands, knowing that the occupation floor was undisturbed, that we were in touch, through this bowl, with its inhabitants, that the archaeology would be wonderful, and this bowl was so beautiful. I wanted everyone to see it; I wanted to shout out loud that we've got a whole vessel right on the floor where it should be (although of course as a professional this is just one more piece of "data"). I felt so very happy, grinning, almost dancing. I relinquished it for others to see, repeating over and over "Please be careful, be very careful with it," and I kept watching it as it moved into the hands of others around me.

20

ANDEAN WAYS

The rodeo

The word was out, although we (foreigners, archaeologists) couldn't understand *how* that could be in a world without phones, email or Twitter. (Of course this isn't really a problem as neighbors and relatives visit constantly by horseback or on foot; Don Beto drives his pickup to and from Santa María; the children bring word back from school. In fact news travels efficiently and quickly among dispersed farmsteads.) The veterinarian, we found out, was coming through the Valle del Cajón at the behest of the newly elected mayor of Santa María. And despite the lack of roads, he was coming to Yutopian; he would walk and ride in, to vaccinate the cattle.

We hadn't seen a cow since we'd been working at Yutopian, and while it's true that archaeologists keep their eyes on the ground, these cows were truly invisible, ranging free in the hills around us. Jorge, his uncles and Ramona each owned several head to make up a herd of perhaps 20, all of which would eventually be sold for beef in Santa María. We had no idea; the Chailes in Yutopian never ate beef because it was too valuable a commodity, and our splendid Yutopian feasts always featured goat meat.

Now, however, Álvaro, Federico, Jorge and Ramona had to locate and round up the cows and bring them down from the hills with the help of only one mare and a pair of yappy dogs, Washingtón and Pluma. We could be of no help at this altitude and at such a strenuous all-day activity, one that started before dawn and ended well after sunset, even wearing our heavy-duty Redwing work boots (while the *lugareños* wore rubber-tire sandals, even in the snow). How they managed this most daunting task is still a mystery, but the roundup was the only occasion when any of the Chailes mentioned, afterward, being tired.

The next day, before any sun found its way into our adobe abode, there were loud unfamiliar wake-up sounds unlike the usual roosters. These were big, painful groaning cries of large animals with big lungs: cows in the corral right outside our window, adults separated from calves, and all mooing, lowing and bellowing to each other across their stone wall divides, the females wanting to be milked and the calves wanting breakfast. Ourselves, we wanted desperately to sleep another half hour.

But there was much to see when we arose: Jorge and the others had put on leather chaps over their homespun pants or patched jeans and carried long loops of homemade sisal rope to accompany the veterinarian out to the "corrals." (These were also the walled gardens which, if it hadn't been winter, would have had corn growing in them.) One by one, each animal had to be lassoed and thrown down so the vet could inject her. To our amazement, each of our archaeological crew members/farmers was also a highly skilled cowhand who accomplished the roping, tackling and throwing of cows efficiently and with elegance, Ramona no less so than her uncles and brother. A cow would be singled out after a brief discussion—each animal individually identifiable to all participants—and its owner would go about bringing it down. Meanwhile, the veterinarian loaded and reloaded his huge needle, wended his way between the lowing animals, and plunged medicine into whichever animal was struggling on the ground, held by one or more of the Chailes (Fig. 33).

By late afternoon, with the bright mountain sun slanting low and the first chill of evening in the air, the veterinarian and the archaeologists were all invited to a celebratory feast that Jorge and Ramona had prepared: roast goat and potatoes, fresh beans and a beautiful drink made from fresh Yutopian peaches. Jorge, the consummate host, had flowers on the long tables laid out for such feasting occasions, and we contributed some wine. To the distress of our sleep patterns, the cows remained in their "corral" for another week, milked by Ramona and Jorge, so there was fresh warm milk those mornings, and rounds of homemade cheese—pressed and aged between flat round rocks—available in the months to come.

Figure 33. Ramona and Jorge vaccinating cows.

Alongside the archaeology, we were learning many Andean lessons during this first field season about gender complementarity, corporate ownership and community responsibility, invisible capital assets, and the many functions of flat round rocks. We were reminded that people didn't eat the same foods — or their favorite foods — all year long, and that feasts were important conclusions to collaborative work.

 # 21

ARGUMENT

Excavation forms

Throughout excavations and analysis at Yutopian we used only slightly modified versions of the same few data-recording forms: one set of forms for recording in the field and monitoring the materials collected by the project, and another in the laboratory for general analysis. A certain self-consciousness underlay my design of these forms because I was already interested in knowledge production, already thinking about categorical observations. Standardized forms are surely a key locus for a broad suite of social practices that mask human agency in producing knowledge and assist in advancing the idea of a value-neutral science. I wasn't eager to perpetuate either this notion or this practice.

Standardized excavation forms are used in most archaeological projects to ensure that a minimum amount of specified information is recorded for each excavation level or observational unit, as crew members are instructed what to observe and what to ignore — that is, what will "count" as data. Forms introduce students to data categories and jog the memory of the experienced digger; they prioritize observations and facilitate inter- and intra-site comparisons of data. Forms streamline unorganized individual observations into categories useful for project purposes; forms promise continuity in the content of knowledge. Yet none of the recorded information ever appears in any recognizable form in a final site report.

Keeping in mind that excavation forms vary considerably from project to project, I reproduce here the basic unit/level form used at Yutopian; it is designed to record information from each 10 cm level of a 2 × 2 m excavation unit, and about 9 or 10 such forms — plus notes, stratigraphic profiles and perhaps special feature maps — would be used for

YUTOPIAN 1998

BOLSAS

Nombre/s_____   ceramics _____

Fecha_____   liticas _____

| estructura |
| unidad |
| nivel |

Profundidad_____   huesos_____

Float samples?_____   Carbón?_____   Otra?_____

N☐

Suelos:

Descripcion:

Hallazgos Especiales?_____
(indicate location on plan)

Fotos: B/W   Slides   Digital   Video

each unit in Estructura 1. Forms are collected in a big loose-leaf binder by structure and excavation unit.

Our unit/level form requires a map to be drawn every time a 10 cm level is finished, with depths of finds and features (including individual stones) marked and mapped. Although the key is not reproduced on the form, crew members learn to use different symbols to plot bone (❑), ceramic (O) and lithics (▲), and to measure in, using tapes and plumb

84

bobs, all finds over 2 cm and all special finds. On the other hand, we generally "guestimate" map locations of smaller redundant finds. The form also inventories what was taken away from the unit level: the number of bags of lithics, ceramics and bone collected; whether soil and/or carbon samples were taken (and from where); whether special finds were designated; and what visual recordings were made. Our form also requires a description of the soil and soil changes, usually in simple verbal descriptions since there was much homogeneity of soil across the site. Finally, the brief overall description of the unit level and what was noted there abbreviates the more extensive notes each excavator makes, so that a particular unit/level form can be recalled and selected more easily.

The Yutopian forms encouraged a rather open-ended format as opposed to projects that require excavators to note which side of an artifact faces upward in the ground, the compass orientation of artifacts and/or the dip from the horizontal plane at which an artifact lies. We also required little artifact classification in the field, whereas other forms ask crew members to recognize and specify distinct artifact classes (not simply raw material) for mapping in the field. Forms are kept simple, not only because crew members are also keeping field journals, but also because of the enormous variability of finds we encounter, in contrast for instance to forms used on Paleo-Indian sites (Gero n.d.) where the diversity of finds is much reduced, the overall occupations less dense, and single artifacts carry greater evidential weight. Additionally, we balanced note taking against how much we could excavate in a season, made more complicated by the scheduling of North American and Argentinean academic calendars and by the climatic conditions in a temperate upland landscape.

Thus the forms we design and press into service to record and preserve our observations in a rigorous and comparative format nevertheless cannot be considered innocent, unproblematic accounts of what was "found." Rather, these instruments directly reflect the sites we work at and are responsive to a wide range of conditioning factors; they do not simply record what we see but also anticipate or forecast what we will encounter.

Filling out forms, assigning artifact identities, and quantifying the locations of finds and features "make data" out of potentially conflicting and ambiguous meanings (Holtorf 2002). Problematic interpretations are denied; we record neither the discussions that precede assignments to an artifact class nor the discussions that accompany demarcations of feature boundaries. Once entered on the forms, the social practices of "doing science" are already masked in favor of final "formal" accounts that emphasize certainty.

Forms also make no provision for contextualizing interpretations in time or space. For instance, the same unit/level form is used for the upper levels of excavation units when we frequently know little or nothing about a local context, and then again for lower levels, where successively more information is fed into our interpretations. The progressive knowledge contexts in which we work are stripped away (except for the indexing date) as data are "form-alized." Similarly, the order in which units or test pits are excavated, or the particular season we happen to be working in, or the point at which some interpretive conclusion is reached and circulated to crew members—all these factors constitute an ever-changing knowledge context that affects meanings assigned on our forms . . . yet all meanings and encodings on forms are accepted as stable and invariant for any and all moments—and any and all contexts—in which the recording was done. Our completed unit/level sheets produce a decontextualized and finalized set of observations sheared from their production matrix as our knowledge takes *form*.

Because formal records obscure the settings in which the recorded observations were situated, standardized field form information is very hard to read by others not involved in the project. To read old files unambiguously, one must apply a knowledge of the site, the period, the region, the director, the crew, the author of the forms, the organization of the project and its procedures, and the purposes for which the forms were maintained (after Garfinkle 1967). That is, field forms create data that are largely internal to the scope of the project while at the same time contradictorily displaying the generalized features of decontextualized facts. Reading field documentation, instead of revealing what was contained in an excavation unit, presupposes that knowledge for a correct reading.

We could go further. Once all recording sheets are collected in a set of notebooks on a shelf, this virtually *becomes* the site, and the site can only be acted upon and witnessed as the series of excavation recording forms plus some visuals. The artifacts now "belong to" discrete excavation levels within which homogeneity prevails and between which distinctions are maintained. Henceforth, all interpretations of past lifeways will be marked with the characteristics of the forms used to "form" them.

Three more things to note about the central position of forms in archaeology: First, unit/level forms set the pace for and produce behavior, coordinating and alternating actions of digging, observing, negotiating fact boundaries and inscribing. Excavators dig to fill out the forms, while the forms coordinate the timing and sequencing of the various activities and instruments and personnel who interact around a given excavation unit. ("Fetch the photographer." "I'm going to get a bucket to take a float sample." "We need more forms!")

Second, the use of forms constitutes a system for direct, empirical witnessing, a personalized pledge of what was encountered and verified in the field, which is the mark of Western science (Shapin and Schaffer 1985). In archaeology, the empirical claims of science to a universal, observable objectivity are especially critical since the context is destroyed through excavation. However compromised the future use of the records may be, the formal records stand as a documented, signed testimony to "what once was" in terms of the context that produced and defined them.

Finally, the practice of using standardized archaeological records demarcates and formalizes interaction across the social and economic boundaries of the excavation hierarchy. On one side, the (gendered male) project director and supervisors participate in an academic reward system based on prestige and gain authority from the authorship of their work. On the other side, the (ungendered) student or professional digger, regardless of the centrality of their work, excavates for money or for academic requirements; they are not identified in the knowledge production nor do they gain authority by their efforts (Edgeworth 1991:51). Thus the completing of the project forms reiterates status and enables the handing over of information to entitled authorities, and affirms and permits—in bodily practice as well as in logical structure—the project hierarchy to operate. Information-bearing forms become a commodity that now belongs to the project administrators and stands timelessly for knowledge.